LEARNING

AS A

WAY

OF

BEING

PETER B. VAILL

LEARNING

AS A

WAY

OF

BEING

Strategies
for Survival
in a
World of
Permanent
White Water

JOSSEY-BASS
A Wiley Company
www.josseybass.com

Published by Jossey-Bass
A Wiley Imprint
989 Market Street, San Francisco, CA 94103-1741   www.josseybass.com

Jossey-Bass books and products are available through most bookstores. To contact Jossey-Bass directly call our Customer Care Department within the U.S. at 800-956-7739, outside the U.S. at 317-572-3986, or fax 317-572-4002.

Jossey-Bass also publishes its books in a variety of electronic formats. Some content that appears in print may not be available in electronic books.

Library of Congress Cataloging-in-Publication Data

Vaill, Peter B.
    Learning as a way of being : strategies for survival in a world of permanent white water / Peter B. Vaill.
        p.   cm.—(The Jossey-Bass business and management series)
    Includes bibliographical references and index.
    ISBN 0-7879-0246-2 (alk. paper)
    1. Executives—Training of.   2. Management—Study and teaching.
  3. Organizational learning.   I. Title.   II. Series.
    HD30.4.V33   1996
    658.4'07124—dc20   95-48137

Printed in the United States of America
FIRST EDITION
HB Printing   20 19 18 17 16 15 14 13 12 11

The Jossey-Bass
Business & Management Series

Contents

. . . .

Preface

This book is about living and working in a productive and healthy way in the extremely turbulent environments of modern organizations. The economist's "firm" isn't so firm anymore, and behind that truth are the innumerable stories of rapid change that all managers are experiencing. This book takes all this change, chaotic as it is, very seriously. I argue that we have barely begun to understand what these rates of change mean for our daily work.

I am thinking primarily of managerial leaders in this book, but the conditions I talk about affect everyone, regardless of job title. I hope the thoughts I have about learning to live more comfortably with these conditions will be relevant to anyone who is interested in organizational life and organizational effectiveness.

This book has been many years in the making. I think it had been under way long before I was even aware of it. I had the privilege to begin my teaching career in the early 1960s, a period of extraordinary ferment in higher education and adult education, marked chiefly by the concept of "relevance"—the determination to make education of all kinds more relevant to the world we live in and to the particular challenges we face as leaders, as employees, as parents, and as citizens. My basic ideas about the educational process were challenged and profoundly stimulated by the ferment of the sixties, as happened to so many thousands of other educators as well. And I had one additional advantage, if one was needed—my subject matter had already committed me to relevance. I was beginning a career as an educator of men and women for professional positions of managerial leadership. Therefore, I was helping them learn about organizations, human motivation, group behavior, communication and interpersonal relations, the process of change, and the challenges of the rapidly changing social, political, economic, and technological environment. Moreover, I had been privileged in my own graduate education to be exposed to a tradition of thinking about managerial leadership that focused on the *interrelation* of abstract knowledge and practical skill. Somehow, an effective educator of managerial leaders was supposed to guide learners not only to acquire useful theoretical ideas about managerial leadership but also to grow and develop in their actual ability to *do* that task. In addition, over the longer term, I as an educator was responsible for producing new knowledge, not just for its own sake but to contribute to the actual improvement of managerial practice.

I have spent the succeeding thirty-plus years in a somewhat schizophrenic mode, given the nature of my training and the decade in which I began my own practice as an educator. Perhaps "schizophrenic" is too strong a word—but perhaps not! In any event, the split I felt was between the fairly well-developed ideology of keeping theory and practice together in management education on the one hand and, on the other hand, the to me increasingly obvious fact that the prevailing forms of education for managerial leadership did not seem to be contributing very much to the improvement of managerial practice, either at the level of individual learners or in the management profession at large. In management education, we were talking about it ad nauseam, and we were letting the learners who came to our management schools and our adult workshops believe that they were getting a carefully crafted balance between theory and practice, but more and more I came to feel that they were not. The academization of education for managerial leadership was powerfully underway, fed by three trends—two having to do with subject matter and one with enrollment.

The two subject matter trends involved the rethinking of managerial leadership in two not always compatible ways: one trend was to reframe managerial situations and problems in sophisticated mathematical terms, thus requiring coursework in quantitative methods that went far beyond anything that had been seen or even imagined in management education before. The other subject matter trend was to see organizations and managerial leaders as objects of rigorous social science and thus to bring academic psychology and sociology into the forefront of management education. Owing to these trends, managerial leadership came to be seen as a fertile and exciting field of application for two academic disciplines that were already highly developed, and not enough educators asked the obvious but extremely difficult and seemingly iconoclastic question: Why do we think managerial leadership is a phenomenon that sophisticated mathematics and social science apply to?

I have been one, along with a few others, who has been asking this question in a variety of ways, but I have not been asking it sweepingly enough, and I have not been asking it insistently enough. One reason I have not is the third trend in education for managerial leadership: we have been in an exploding market. Education for management has been the Cabbage Patch doll of higher education since the late 1960s. Inquiry into the meaning and value of management education and training tended to be seen as mere complaint and was ignored in the explosion of enrollments. It is not widely known, but on many college campuses, the business school is the largest degree-granting unit (although in the 1990s, that robust enrollment growth has plateaued). Furthermore, students who wanted a management degree were not sensitive to the subtlety of the theory-versus-practice issue. They arrived ready to take their castor oil. Everybody "knew" business was supposed to be a boring subject, so when it turned out to be so, no one complained. The lucrative job market of the 1970s and 1980s supposedly made the pain acceptable, as the price of admission to that market.

In the face of the bull market for management education, questions that asked what managerial leadership is really about and what the learning process for it ought to be were, ironically, seen as too academic. Those of us asking the questions usually gained verbal assent to our concerns from other faculty, but no one shifted his or her behavior very much.

This pattern began to change for me in the mid 1980s, as I began to think about the true amount of turbulence and change managerial leaders were dealing with in their organizations. The more the pace of change quickened and the chaotic feel of organizations increased, the more absurd a structured academic approach to teaching managerial leadership seemed to become.

This turbulence, this *permanent white water* of modern organizations, is one of the core ideas of this book, and it dates in my thinking from 1985. I first developed it in *Managing as a Performing Art* (1989a). Almost in passing in that book, I devoted a few pages to the phenomenon of "what we are like when we are playing a game we have never played before" (pp. 23–28), for that is what permanent white water creates: an environment of continual newness. I knew at the time that this phenomenon had much deeper implications for managerial leaders and the way they develop than I was then able to go into. In the succeeding months, I crystallized the problem faced by these leaders as one of continual learning under constantly changing conditions. I had discovered what many others had discovered already—that continual learning is a requirement of the modern environment.

But what is continual learning? The beginnings of an answer to that question are what it has taken this book to develop. It turns out that the answer involves a critical examination of what educators and others concerned with management development already know and don't know about continual learning as a result of their years of indoctrination in the school system, and it requires that we develop a new philosophy of continual learning for the organizational world that is evolving. *The primary purpose of this book is to make the nature of continual learning for managerial leadership real and not just the cliché of congressional testimonies and keynote addresses at meetings of educators.*

So this book is a manifesto. It is intended to intensify the debate over how we should be conducting our education and training for managerial leadership. As such, it is designed to appeal to professional educators, both the experienced and those in training, to those concerned in any way with management education and development, and most of all to practicing managers, for it is their learning needs and learning practices that I am most concerned with in this book. I *know* professional educators are not doing a very good job of meeting these needs. Maybe practicing managerial leaders can help me say so even more incisively than I have been able to in these pages.

A Brief Preview of the Contents

Learning as a Way of Being opens with a reprise and an updating of my thinking about permanent white water. This notion was the seminal idea of my previous book, but there is a great deal more to be said about it. In fact, in that earlier book, I never did really spell out what I meant by the kinds of events I call permanent white water. The present Introduction describes these events and explores the meaning of the idea much more thoroughly.

Chapter One picks up on the note sounded at the end of the Introduction—that the best means of coping with nonstop white water in organizations is through effective learning. Then I step back to ask how well prepared we are as learners for the kind of learning we have to do in permanent white water. The basic argument is that the formal school system, which I call *institutional learning*, has ill-prepared us for the messy learning world we inhabit as practicing managerial leaders and other kinds of professionals. The formal school system is shown to be primarily a control system, not a truly educational system in which liberation of the mind and spirit of learners is the primary objective. Furthermore, the formal school system has profoundly influenced so-called adult education—the kinds of experiences being provided in the world of work for men and women who are trying to do the learning that is so essential. If we think learning is so important, Chapter One concludes, we had better rethink the kind of learning, in content, form, and underlying philosophy, that we are talking about.

In Chapter Two, I undertake that rethinking. This chapter contains my core learning and educational philosophy, which I call *learning as a way of being.* That learning *is* a way of being is, after all, not such a radical idea. Few would quarrel with the notion that to be a human being is to be a continual learner all of one's life. But institutional learning, as I argue in Chapter Two, has prevented us from understanding what such continual learning can be. Learning as a way of being is viewed as a system of seven qualities, each of which is an aspect of the kind of learning that is needed for an environment of permanent white water. While none of the seven qualities is absolutely original, at least a couple of them are learning process qualities we do not hear very much about. The philosophy behind mainstream institutional learning is usually indifferent to these seven qualities and sometimes is outright hostile toward them. Furthermore, this chapter portrays learning as a way of being as a *system* of these seven qualities, which depend on each other for their effectiveness. Educators who have tried to implement versions of one or two of these qualities at a time have learned about this interdependency the hard way.

In Chapters Three, Four, Five, and Six, I take four topics and apply concepts of learning as a way of being to them. What might systems learning as a way of being be like (Chapter Three)? Or "leaderly" learning as a way of being (Chapter Four)? How and why must cultural learning as a way of being be cultural unlearning as a way of being (Chapter Five)? And what might spiritual learning as a way of being be like (Chapter Six)? I chose the topics of systems, leadership, culture, and spirituality because they are enormously rich in their learning potential, and because all four are currently regarded as highly important matters of managerial learning. They do not exhaust the list of topics managers might be learning, though. Topics that might be discussed at a later time include learning information technology, learning sophisticated new financial concepts and techniques, learning total quality and reengineering approaches to improvement, learning new approaches to human resource management and development, and learning more about oneself as a managerial leader and as a person—in short, learning anything of relevance to one's situation in the white water world of contemporary organizations.

I chose the four topics of Chapters Three through Six for another reason as well: none of them is well handled by institutional learning. Each of these topics has an intrinsic character that is either significantly distorted or outright ignored by institutional learning philosophy and practice. If we are really serious about helping men and women in positions of managerial leadership become more knowledgeable and more skillful with these topics, we need to rethink how they can be presented.

My hope is that the reader will use these four "application" chapters as a stimulus and perhaps a loose guide to applying learning as a way of being to any learning process that he or she might choose. I can testify that in each chapter, the process of thinking about the learning challenges posed by the particular subject has led me to major new insights about what is involved in learning that subject. Learning as a way of being opens my eyes to learning challenges, helps me see things that a learner is up against that I had never seen before—and I say this of four subjects that I have been "professing" for years and years. My trust is that the reader will have the same kinds of discoveries about learning challenges as he or she proceeds to apply learning as a way of being to other subjects.

The Epilogue takes the critique of institutional learning to another level and sketches a deeper problem with formal learning systems than is reached by the previous chapters. The philosophy and practice of institutional learning contain profound and far-reaching assumptions about the nature of knowledge itself—assumptions that in my experience most educators are either indifferent to or unaware of. The subject of the Epilogue deserves book-length analysis at least. The sketch here is intended merely to point beyond this book and to punctuate the seriousness of the issues I have discussed here.

Acknowledgments

Given that this book is a personal philosophical critique of my profession of the last thirty-five years and that it argues for fairly dramatic change in the way that all of us who educate, coach, or consult to managerial leaders work with those leaders, I find myself in the position of wishing to thank virtually everyone I have ever worked with for helping me crystallize the ideas I present here. I know that many of my friends and colleagues will recognize things they are saying and doing in these pages. Some of those whose philosophies and practices bother me may recognize themselves, too! But the overall spirit of this book is constructive, even though, in Chapter One in particular, I must be highly critical of one of the dominant institutions and social movements of the last two hundred years—our formal educational system.

I wish to say clearly here that I am very aware of the many management educators and trainers who agree with me philosophically, and I am always stimulated and delighted when I come across a program that tries to be true to the spirit of learning and to contribute to the demise of the spirit of indoctrination and control that is so prevalent. But to the many innovators, known and unknown, I also have to pose this set of questions, based on my own failures and on years of observation: To what extent does your innovation still collude with the institutional learning system described in Chapter One? To what extent are you still not helping the learner get over the hump of dependence on you as the Keeper of the Right Answer? To what extent are you being too cautious?

There is an even deeper set of questions, which it is not fair to ask any single educational innovator but which we somehow have to come to grips with: How is it that we keep "rediscovering America" when we discuss truly learner-centered philosophy and practice? Why aren't the exciting experiments that have been tried more contagious? Why does the system exhaust and demoralize, indeed demote and decertify, so many of the innovators?

So, while wishing to thank so many people who have stimulated my thinking over the years, the main people I want to thank are the learners themselves. They are the ones who put up with the ponderous and pointless practices of the old system. And it is they who never fail to respond with enthusiasm and creativity when a professional educator does happen to come up with an innovation that honors and enriches their learning as a way of being.

Johns Creek   Peter B. Vaill
Lusby, Maryland
February 1996

for Stanley and Deborah,
Ellie and Hart,
Emily, David, and Andrew,
and Timothy and April,
who write with their lives

The Author

· ·

Peter B. Vaill is professor of human systems and director of the Ph.D. program at the School of Business and Public Management, George Washington University. He is the former dean of this school. He has also served on the management faculties of the University of Connecticut and the University of California, Los Angeles, and as visiting professor of organizational behavior at the Stanford Business School. He holds a B.A. degree (1958) from the University of Minnesota, an M.B.A. degree (1960) from the Harvard Business School, and a D.B.A. degree (1964) in organizational behavior, also from the Harvard Business School.

His special fields of interest include strategic management, organization development, cross-cultural management, managerial learning, and leadership, with special attention to the spiritual problems of modern organizational leaders. His essay "Toward a Behavioral Theory of High Performing Systems" (1972) proposed the first contemporary theory of what has come to be called organizational excellence. In 1985, Vaill was described in *Training and Development Journal* as one of the top ten organization development specialists in the United States.

He has worked with many well-known corporations and with most of the major agencies of the U.S. government as well as with many universities, health systems, and professional associations. His work has taken him to Great Britain, Germany, Belgium, Holland, Switzerland, the Scandinavian countries, Egypt, Iran, and Japan.

Vaill's articles and book chapters include "The Purposing of High Performing Systems" (*Organizational Dynamics*, Fall 1982); "Process Wisdom for a New Age" (*Transforming Work*, edited by J. Adams, 1985); "Integrating the Diverse Directions of the Behavioral Sciences," (*Human Systems Development*, by R. Tannenbaum, N. Margulies, F. Massarik, and Associates, 1985); "O.D. as a Scientific Revolution," (*Contemporary Organization Development*, edited by D. D. Warrick, 1985); "Seven Process Frontiers for Organization Development" (*The Emerging Practice of Organization Development*, by A. Drexler and W. Sikes, 1989); "Executive Development as Spiritual Development" (*Appreciative Management and Leadership*, by S. Srivastva, D. L. Cooperrider, and Associates, 1990); "Visionary Leadership" (*The Portable MBA in Management*, edited by A. Cohen, 1993); and "Notes on Running an Organization" (*Journal of Management Inquiry*, June 1992). A book of his essays, *Managing as a Performing Art: New Ideas for a World of Chaotic Change*, was published by Jossey-Bass in 1989.

Vaill is a member of the Academy of Management, the Organizational Behavior Teaching Society, the National Organization Development Network, and the Chesapeake Bay O.D. Network. He has been a speaker at the national and regional programs of these societies many times. He is also a charter member of the MetaNetwork, an international computer conferencing system. From 1985 to 1988, he was editor of *Organizational Dynamics*, the journal of the American Management Association. Since 1990, he has been a member of the board of governors of the Center for Creative Leadership.

Introduction

· ·

An Ordinary Day on the River

Living in a World
of Permanent White Water

I t is 6:15 in the morning, and you are finishing a cup of coffee while glancing through the paper before you get in your car and head for the airport, an estimated forty-minute drive at this hour. You're due for a 10:30 A.M. business meeting in a city 500 or so miles away, and you're on a 7:45 flight that should get you there in plenty of time to take a cab into the city for your meeting. After the meeting, there will probably be lunch and some follow-up conversations in the afternoon. You booked your return ticket on the 6:00 P.M. flight, allowing for the heavy afternoon traffic between where your meeting will be and the airport. You expect to be back home by 8:30 this evening.

· · · · · · · ·

The foregoing scenario was deliberately uneventful. Presumably, it happens just like this millions of times a day, year after year after year. But of course, it does not always happen as expected and intended, for all kinds of unplanned things can occur, causing lost time and other kinds of aggravation. Unexpectedly nice things can happen, too, but they don't seem to happen as often, and in any case, they don't usually create the coping problems presented by thunderstorms, lost luggage, and overbooked return flights.

As we plan and go through experiences like this day trip, we are aware to varying degrees of the assumptions we are making that things will go according to plan. Most of us are pretty aware, for example, that the allowances we make for road traffic congestion can be totally wrong on a given rainy morning and that planes can be delayed not only by weather but by mechanical problems. We make other assumptions we are perhaps less aware of: for example, that we will not be mistaken for terrorists and detained for an hour by airport security guards; that our understanding of the day, time, and city of the meeting is correct; or that the labor unions governing pilots, flight attendants, mechanics, baggage handlers, and police will not pick this morning for a wildcat strike. At some level of awareness, we know these things *could* happen, but we are not focused on them.

Even though we are quite aware of some assumptions, and would become aware of many others if they were violated, it is unlikely that many of us have an overall grasp of the mass of assumptions our unremarkable one-day business trip involves. What if we actually sat down and began listing the systems that have to work more or less within designed limits in order for us to do what we want to do, in this case, have our one-day business trip go off as intended? Let me name a few (with the awareness that each of these "systems" can be broken down into a host of subsystems that have their own degrees of complexity, fragility, and unpredictability).

- Our own psychological and biological systems

- The home systems via which we wake up, wash, dress, and feed ourselves

- A family system tranquil enough for us to proceed with our plans for the day rather than spending time problem solving with spouse, kids, or other family members

- Our personal transportation system

- All the traffic control systems governing our trip to the airport

- The airport parking system

- The system that ticketed us and that generates a boarding pass

- The airport security system

- Essential passenger convenience systems at the airport, such as food services, money machines, telephones, and so on

- All the systems that deliver an airplane, on time, ready to fly, to our departure gate

- The plane boarding system

- The air traffic control system and other electronic communication systems

- The biological and psychological systems of all those involved in the plane's flying performance

- Weather systems, and the human systems through which we understand them

- The systems in the other aircraft whose flight paths and other actions could affect the performance of our aircraft

- The same systems that affected our departure from our home airport as they affect our arrival at our destination airport

- The transportation system into our destination city

- The physical and social systems through which the meeting occurs and runs smoothly

- Meeting support systems such as duplication, fax, and secretarial services

- All the systems we used to get to the meeting as we use them again to get home from the meeting

- The technical systems (infrastructure), like water and power supplies and telephones services and roads, upon which all the systems mentioned above rest and which in turn rest on systems of politics and economics that we assume will endure

This list sketches the working world, the *macrosystem,* of millions of people—both those who are using the systems for their own purposes and those who are operating the systems as their jobs. The miracle is that this macrosystem, and many others like it, works as well as it does. Most of the time, through slack in the system, the users' anticipation of problems, the operators' innovativeness and commitment to their mission, and luck, we more or less get done what it is we are trying to get done.

However, the complex contingencies and interdependencies of the systems of the modern world warrant a much closer look than we tend to give them. In an earlier book (Vaill, 1989a), I used the expression *permanent white water* to describe the complex, turbulent, changing environment in which we are all trying to operate.[1] The macrosystem of air transport and associated ground systems is a perfect example of the interrelationship of human attitudes and activities with mechanical and electronic functions and natural-world events, an interaction in which permanent white water is found in abundance and in which extraordinary demands are made on the people operating and using these complex sociotechnical systems. I believe we need to understand these system conditions and these

---

1. As this book goes to press, "Whitewater" has become the name for the collection of events, rumors, and investigatory processes surrounding President and Mrs. Clinton's real-estate investment in the 1980s in Arkansas. This is a quite different meaning from the one offered in this book, although, ironically, the Whitewater Affair has plunged the Clinton White House into what I call permanent white water.

demands on people a great deal more thoroughly than we now do. To that end, this book has been written. I take as given that today's complex, interdependent, and unstable systems require continual imaginative and creative initiatives and responses by those living and working in them—and especially by those leading and managing them. My central thesis is that

- Our continual imaginative and creative initiatives and responses to systems are, in fact, *continual learning;*[2] in other words, continual learning is what we are seeing as we observe people acting in complex situations.

- We need to consider carefully what we need to learn about continual learning to live productively and comfortably in our macrosystems.

- We need also to consider whether we are as prepared to engage in continual learning as we need to be, and if so, how we go about engaging in it.

In this first chapter, I will say quite a bit more about the sources and effects of permanent white water conditions, building on my earlier discussion and the work of others. My real concern throughout is what we will be able to make of these conditions as leaders and managers and as employees, parents, and citizens.

The Social Nature of Operating Systems

Let me return for a few moments to the example of the interaction of multiple systems in the simple business trip. I said the miracle is

---

2.   I have chosen the word *continual* over the word *continuous* because *continual*, as H. W. Fowler points out, describes something that "either is always going on or recurs at short intervals and never comes (or is regarded as never coming) to an end." Whereas *continuous* describes the situation "in which no break occurs between the beginning and the (not necessarily or even presumably long-deferred) end" (1965, p. 109). It is *continual* that quite exactly describes the kind of learning I have in mind.

that this macrosystem and others like it work as well as they do. Now consider why these systems work as well as they do. It is certainly true that they are typically well designed against carefully formulated objectives and that they employ sophisticated technologies throughout. There is no doubt that they meet significant needs in society and that we all have an incentive to keep them going, especially those that supply us with power, light, and food.

But these systems are not machines. They are not merely rational technical achievements. They are *social* systems as well. In Trist's landmark formulation, they are "socio-technical systems" (Trist, Higgin, Murray, and Pollock, 1963). These systems run because at millions of operational points, human will and human judgment are exercised, usually on behalf of the systems' objectives. The will and judgment are exercised both by those who operate the systems and by those who use them. *Both* the baggage handler and the passenger take actions that are intended to get the passenger's bags correctly tagged and on the plane on time. Obviously, therefore, if the requisite human will and judgment are not applied at the right times and in the right ways in a system, it will not operate the way it is supposed to. The bags will get lost or damaged. The baggage-handling portion of the macrosystem will have failed.

Permanent white water metaphorically defines the difficult conditions under which people exercise their will and judgment within society's macrosystems. Virtually every person acting within the various systems that support a business trip is coping with a continuing stream of changes that makes operating his or her part of the system anything but routine. All these people are under continuing pressure to improve performance and control costs. They are all confronted constantly with new methods and technologies. Every one of them is working with new people in the system all the time, and the mix of people of different nationalities, ethnicities, religions, and gender is also increasing. All of them are experiencing great stress and complexity outside the job, living as they do in a society with burgeoning social problems such as drug abuse, crime, consumer debt, family conflicts, pollution, and racial and ethnic conflict. Despite the stress they are under, they are all being urged to innovate, to look for ways to improve the operation of the system, to upgrade their own skills, and to work more effectively with each other. They are being asked to view their jobs and themselves in career terms, that is, to assume they will be working in this system indefinitely. In effect, even as they personally experience the ongoing impact of changes introduced by others, of permanent white water, they are creating permanent white water for others by the changes they themselves introduce. Turbulence and instability are woven into the macrosystem; they are not just things that happen to it from the outside.

It is probably a safe bet to say that all the various participants in this macrosystem are trying to get their parts of it running smoothly, constantly looking ahead to a time when things will settle down ("and we'll be able to get some *work* done around here"), but none are succeeding except temporarily. Why? *Because it is the nature of macrosystems to upset all attempts to get subparts to run smoothly.* We yearn for the operation that runs without problems; we hold ourselves and others responsible for bringing it about; we carve out a piece of turf that we think we can control and defend it ferociously; we gnash our teeth when we fail to achieve the stability and tranquility we are seeking. (Murphy's Law—"Anything that can go wrong, will go wrong"—is best understood as an anguished cry, not a philosophical observation.) Rarely, however, do we ask ourselves if maybe our model of the macrosystem and how it is supposed to work might be wrong in the first place. Although more than twenty years ago, Russell Ackoff (1974) suggested that it is system members' attempts to get subparts to run smoothly that is a principal cause of conflicts, inefficiencies, and breakdowns in the macrosystem. People are inadvertently impeding each other, canceling out each other's efforts.

The metaphor of permanent white water asserts that the model of a smooth-running macrosystem and component parts is intrinsically invalid. *The system is not a clock of mechanically engineered parts.* The design specifications for how the macrosystem *should* run cannot take account of all the changes being introduced into it by people inside and outside. The actual operating macrosystem is a joint product of its rational design specifications and the emergent changes, intended and unintended, that occur during system operation. In particular, *the operating macrosystem is profoundly affected by the quality of human will and judgment that is concurrently present throughout the system.* The design specifications pertain to initial conditions; they cannot predict how the pervasive exercise of human will and judgment will modify the system. Just think of the kinds of changes in the air transport macrosystem that even the most casual traveler will have noted: new airports, new concourses, new air traffic control systems, new ticketing and baggage-handling arrangements, new security systems, new approaches to boarding planes, new approaches to feeding passengers and providing for their safety aloft, and of course, new planes themselves. There are innumerable changes in addition that are invisible to the traveler but acutely real for those who have to learn to operate the systems that contain them. The traveler, too, is constantly experimenting: for example, with different itineraries and schedules, different kinds of luggage, and different routes to and from the airport.

Some of these changes are official, meaning that they go through a careful design review process and are incorporated at least somewhat planfully into the system (although designs and plans are no guarantee that changes will not create major disturbances). But just as many changes are informal—shortcuts, innovations, Band-Aids of one sort or another that individuals and groups apply to the system flow to solve the local problems they experience. These spontaneous innovations create a lot of unanticipated permanent white water for others upstream or downstream in the system. Valuable innovations are the positive result of this age of individual "empowerment" that we live in, but the cost is likely to be continuing system disturbances owing to members' nonstop tinkering. However, because the tinkering can be seen as members' way to cope with the stresses and contradictions they experience in the system's operation, we have to permit as much local innovation as we can. For if members and users of the system do not do well in coping with stress and change, the macrosystem (dependent on their will and judgment) will degrade, even to the point of collapse.

Faced with these conditions, it is understandable that some systems designers should introduce more controls on innovation, more reports to fill out, and more committees to clear before a modification can be adopted. Their impulse to control works against innovation at the operational level, of course, and is experienced by those with their hands on the equipment as a proliferation of red tape; in effect, an increase in the permanent white water. Thus, at any moment, the system is drawing out of both its operators and its nominal designers/controllers behavior that increases the complexity and fragility of the system, and just as importantly, frays people's nerves and punishes their efforts to make the system run smoothly.

Another strategy system designers and controllers use to defend against degradation is to remove the human component by automating the system. This, however, can never be more than a local and sharply circumscribed solution. There will always be a larger *socio*technical macrosystem containing the automated component, and in this larger system, human will and judgment will continue to be decisive. We cannot escape the consequences of human suffering and ineptitude in the permanent white water of our systems.

This is not a book that is primarily about the theory of these turbulent macrosystems per se or about how systems designers can design them to run more smoothly. Rather, I direct our focus toward the *feel* of these systems to those who live in them, work in them, and use them and toward the kinds of demands they place on mind, body, and spirit. An underlying assumption of this approach is that the theory of these systems, interesting and powerful as it is, does not replace on-the-spot wisdom, creativity, and steadiness when things are going wrong at a particular moment, and white water is splashing in all directions. (Some readers may be reminded of chaos theory at this point. Chaos theory and permanent white water concern the same phenomena, but the descriptions and explanations in chaos theory are about the white water itself, not about the feelings and reactions of those who are experiencing it directly. Chaos theory may eventually produce guides to action for social systems, but it has not yet done so in detail.)

This is not the place for an extended digression on the possibility that a scientific understanding of social systems cannot successfully replace human common sense and a form of human consciousness that when it acts in such systems transcends science. Rather, I will simply observe that so far, systems science has not rescued leaders and managers from needing the ability to "Band-Aid," "muddle through," "learn as we go along," "fly by the seat of our pants," and "keep our fingers crossed." So, as a practical matter, I take survival in permanent white water to be, for the foreseeable future, less a matter of applied science and more a matter of some other kinds of consciousness and skill. One way of viewing this book is as a reflection on that consciousness and skill.

The Characteristics of Permanent White Water

There are five intertwining characteristics of what I have been calling permanent white water that taken together capture the feel of permanent white water conditions.

1. *Permanent white water conditions are full of surprises.* This is perhaps the most obvious characteristic of permanent white water conditions—the continual occurrence of problems that are not expected, problems that are not "supposed" to happen. The original Saturn car, a brand new automobile that was the object of pos-

sibly more thought and investment of resources and state-of-the-art management thinking than any other project in the history of the automotive industry, was not supposed to be the immediate object of a recall. Not that recalls are unimaginable or that we are paralyzed when the need for one occurs; no. Recalls just are not supposed to happen when that much care has been devoted to a car's design and production. This does not mean that a recall won't exist somewhere on some systems designer's chart of all possible outcomes. Rather, it means that all those involved in the design, manufacture, distribution, and ultimate use of the car are not expecting a recall to be necessary. It is not in their plans, and when it occurs, their actions in response are sometimes guided by a back-up plan, but just as often, their response is a matter of ad hoc invention. The examples of such surprises are endless, whether in manufacturing and distribution, in the unexpected behavior of economic factors, in the surprising things customers or employees can do, or in such acts of God as the 1991 volcanic eruption in the Philippines. Surprises need not be negative or disastrous either in order to be extremely taxing to those involved; witness the stresses placed on such companies as Apple Computer, Nike, and Coleco by the explosive growth in sales of the original personal computers, athletic shoes during the jogging boom, and Cabbage Patch dolls.

2. *Complex systems tend to produce novel problems.* This second characteristic of permanent white water conditions usually occurs along with the first one of surprise. Novel problems are those that are not only not anticipated but also not even imagined by those concerned with the system. Every executive can tell these stories; some are horrifying, like the ones about the nature and consequences of the AIDS epidemic, but just as many are amusing, like the one about the word "naval" spelled with an "e" on the 1990 graduation diplomas at the U.S. Naval Academy or (as was reported to me by an executive in the highly competitive long-distance telephone industry) the one about the miles of fiber optic cable laid in the West rendered useless after gophers unexpectedly developed a

taste for cable insulation. We might hypothesize that the large macrosystems of modern society, with their innumerable delicate interdependencies and closely calibrated operating specifications, are actually novelty *generators*, that it is in their nature to throw up problems no one has seen before or even imagined. The feeling of novelty is captured in comments we have all heard dozens of times from executives in modern organizations: "It's a whole new ball game." "It's business as *unusual!*" "If there is any rule book at all, we're writing it as we go."

3.   *Permanent white water conditions feature events that are "messy" and ill-structured* (Ackoff, 1974, p. 21). These events do not present themselves in neat packages that can easily be delegated or farmed out to a consultant. An unexpected lawsuit, for example, has ramifications in all directions, affecting a wide range of loosely related policies and practices in an organization. Dealing with the meaning and consequences of such an event, then, involves people in a wide range of operations, operations that have their own imperatives and contingencies and that may be simultaneously feeling the effects of other white water events. "Everything's connected to everything else," is an intellectually luxurious insight when made outside such systems but a minefield for those who are trying to resolve something in particular within a system. One reason "systems thinking" is such a difficult mentality to acquire is that we often do not *want* everything to be connected to everything else. We want relatively simple cause-effect chains so that we can "take action" that will "get results." (I deal further with this issue in Chapter Three.)

4.   *White water events are often extremely costly.* They may be expensive in terms of dollars or in terms of some other scarce resource in the system. An *Exxon Valdez* oil spill costs hundreds of millions of dollars out of pocket and the same amount in man-hours devoted to the problem, and that is before any reparations are paid to injured parties. The cost of misreading of what the public wants a soft drink to taste like (as happened to Coca-Cola) or the cost of

responding responsibly to a product poisoning crisis (as happened to Johnson & Johnson with Tylenol) can run into the tens and hundreds of millions of dollars. Worse than the sheer magnitude of cost is the difficulty of planning and budgeting to cope with the problem and correct the damage. Surprising, novel, and messy problems unfold and feed on themselves in their ramifications, rather than displaying their implications all at once. The federal bailout of U.S. savings and loan institutions offers an excellent example of the near impossibility of understanding all at once the magnitude of a highly complex situation. One can only keep revising cost estimates upward and time lines farther out into the future as the dimensions of the mess unfold. Cost can be measured in absolute terms (as in some of the examples cited), but cost can also be relative. Even when the absolute magnitude of cost is not that great, permanent white water events are costly in the sense that the time taken to deal with them must be diverted from other pressing issues and is acutely felt as a diversion of time and resources. In general, we may say that these events are extremely *obtrusive*. In their messiness, costliness, and ramifications, they simply cannot be ignored.

5.   *Permanent white water conditions raise the problem of recurrence*. They make us ask whether a particular white water event could have been anticipated, whether anything like it will occur again, whether a new system should be designed to forestall this type of event in the future. These events increase the red tape, in other words, as investigations are conducted and conditions that led to the event are reconstructed. Bureaucratic complexities are introduced as various policies and functions are created to prevent the problem from recurring. While such protections may be undoubtedly valuable in some circumstances, it is important to understand that no number of anticipatory mechanisms can forestall the next surprising, novel wave in the permanent white water. There is no way the system can be protected against all eventualities without paralyzing it. Events of the sort we have been considering will keep happening indefinitely: while particular events may not recur,

unpreventable recurrence of similar events is a fact of life in the complex and interdependent systems of the modern world.

Our Reactions to Permanent White Water

Permanent white water consists of events that are surprising, novel, messy, costly, and unpreventable. While some people may be moved to debate whether this means the world is in fact becoming more turbulent than it was during, say, World War II or the Great Depression—or the fourteenth century for that matter—the question is probably indeterminable. But that is not the point. It is the subjective feel of these events as much as their objective existence that we are concerned with. Therefore, *the real point is whether experienced executives and others in organizations perceive that what they are trying to do is becoming more complex, problematic, and contingent as time goes on*. With this there seems to be widespread agreement: permanent white water conditions are regularly taking us all out of our comfort zones and asking things of us that we never imagined would be required. Permanent white water means permanent life outside one's comfort zone. The results of Porter and McKibben's timely survey of educational needs of managers are just one example of people's current perceptions. Porter and McKibben report: "Time and again in our interviews we were struck by the almost tangible awe with which middle-age (let alone older-age) and even youngish managers in their late thirties were viewing the rapidity with which their work environments—both outside and within the organization— were changing" (1988, p. 231). Moreover, I and my colleague Eric Dent are in the process of developing an instrument (reproduced in Resource I) to measure the extent to which practicing managers are experiencing a pickup in the pace, complexity, unpredictability, and confusion of work life over the previous five years or so. Preliminary results with three hundred practicing managers show an average score (over twenty-one items) of +2, suggesting that indeed people are *feeling* the white water intensifying. Only about 5 percent of respondents give themselves the maximum score, but so far no one has given himself or herself a negative score, that is, a score indicating that the person's work world was becoming more tranquil.

That we are indeed experiencing high levels of confusion and turbulence can be found right in our everyday organizational language. I have given some examples already. In addition, my students at George Washington University and I found we could quickly generate a large number of familiar phrases about turbulence and confusion that are heard all the time in organizations. People describe other people as "rocking the boat," "going ballistic," "getting hit by friendly fire," "bouncing off the walls," "wandering around in a house of mirrors," "being the blind leading the blind," and "dodging bullets." They talk about "being on a roller coaster," "a see-saw," or "a merry-go-round," about "being in the theater of the absurd," about "rearranging the deck chairs on the *Titanic*." They wonder, "Who's on first?" and "Are the patients running the asylum?" They feel "the situation unravelling," "things coming apart at the seams," "the train leaving the tracks," "a meltdown happening." They see tasks as "Catch-22s" or "Looney Tunes times." They think of events as "spinning out of control" or, at the other extreme, "being dead in the water." They compare their activities to "something in a puzzle palace" or "something out of *Alice in Wonderland*" or "a Keystone Kops movie" and they whistle the theme from *The Twilight Zone*.

These familiar metaphors, and many others the reader will think of, have some themes in common—summed up by the metaphorical observation of a military friend of mine that in the midst of confusion and turbulence, many people's behavior can be described as "all thrust and no vector." These metaphors are reactions to a felt lack of continuity and of direction, the absence of a sense of progress and of cumulative achievement, a lack of coherence and of meaning, and a lack of control. Clearly, permanent white water is not just the facts and events surrounding members of organizations. Permanent white water is the *meaning* we as system members attach to our experiences. We experience both surprising, novel, messy, costly, recurring, and unpreventable events *and* feelings of lack of direction, absence of coherence, and loss of meaning.

Our growing feeling of loss of meaning derives from several sources. White water events often contain a clash of logics and priorities as asserted by various stakeholder groups such as customers, suppliers, owners, competitors, and employees. One wants quantity; another quality. One wants cost control; another bold new investment. One wants to cease and desist; another to redouble effort. In what coherent and convincing terms are we to think about an organizational reengineering (a positive, hopeful signal) that entails a layoff of 25 percent of the hourly and middle-management workforce (a powerful negative signal), both events supposedly a creative response to a Japanese competitor that is itself increasingly manifesting the strains and confusion of permanent white water?

Meaninglessness also derives from the broken promises and disappointments of science and technology. Systems that were supposed to produce more control produce whole new kinds of problems that did not exist before the systems were installed. Cost overruns are chronic; malfunction of delicate technical interfaces is endemic. Is life really easier now that we have, say, a multimedia fax machine—a totally mythical piece of technology that is nonetheless probably only months away from hitting the market? William Barrett (1978) called it "the illusion of technique"—this belief in the power of science and technology to take away problems without adding any contingency, danger, or moral confusion to our lives.

Our own growth, education, increasing sophistication, and knowledge of other cultures and value systems may also be contributing to our feelings of uncertainty and confusion. Relativism may be a more practical and defensible philosophy than absolutism, but at the personal level, the transition from one to the other can nevertheless be agonizing. Who is right in the various debates that are sweeping through societal and organizational life? When we didn't know of these debates or understand the arguments on various sides, perhaps it was easier—albeit more naïve—to think we understood the meaning of our work and our lives. Now we know the various points of view with our heads, but at the level of feeling, are we more serene? "Hang ideas," said Joseph Conrad ([1900] 1931) in a memorable cry of anguish. "They are tramps, vagabonds, knocking at the back door of your mind, each taking a little of your substance, each carrying away some crumb of that belief in a few simple notions you must cling to if you want to live decently and would like to die easy" (p. 43).

Finally, the horrors of the twentieth century have unquestionably contributed to our loss of a sense of meaning. The horrors are not only in the wars, famines, and holocausts occurring on the macro scale but in the atrocities of daily life on our streets and playgrounds and in our offices. Drive-by murder is a horrifying fact in itself, but it is also a metaphor for the casual violence that is being done to our lives and sense of meaning, not only by guns but by layoff slips, voice mail from the truant officer, and cancellation notices from our health insurance companies.

The objective events that are contributing to our loss of a sense of meaning, direction, and control are not going to abate. If anything, they will proliferate and intensify. What, however, of the subjective side? What of our capacity to restore and sustain a sense of meaning in these new chaotic environments? Can we indeed learn to "thrive on chaos," as Tom Peters (1987) suggests? This is one problem to which this book is addressed.

Creating Our Own Permanent White Water

Beyond what happens *to* us, we actually create permanent white water for ourselves and others. Our struggle to restore meaning in our immediate work environments leads us to take actions that may be experienced as white water by others. For one thing, organizational leaders are setting more and more ambitious goals. It is not unusual at all for top management to decree that a productivity increase of 5 to 10 percent per year is expected from an employment level that will shrink by the same amount per year. The ongoing information revolution continues to create apparent opportunities that organizations ignore at their peril. This is the "informating" quality of computerized information systems that Shoshanna Zuboff (1988) has described: the possession of an automated information system does not just enable us to know and do more efficiently the things we did before in a more manual mode. It also teaches us things about our system and its environment that we could not have known without the automated information system, thus causing us to address problems, make decisions, and initiate courses of action that we would never have conceived of before the computer-generated information arrived.

More decentralization also creates more white water because it substantially increases the number of points in a complex system where managers are empowered to take major initiatives without having to go through a lengthy approval process up the line. The net effect is that change is being initiated from many points in the organizational network, not just from the top.

The enormous increase in emphasis on service also creates more white water for everyone. It declares that the quality of the customer relationship will be measured as much by the customer's subjective experience of feeling served as it will by the harder measure of whether a product was delivered to specification. In the service business, service is in the eye of the beholder. If we are serious about service, we are not "done" until the customer says we are done. An emphasis on service asks system members to personalize relations with customers, and that personalization introduces more contingency, more opportunity for surprise and for novelty than existed when service was not a priority. Furthermore, the customer, too, is in permanent white water and would like the product or service supplier not to add to it and, preferably, to reduce it. *Service* means a willingness to absorb the customer's white water. Seen in this light, real determination to be of service is an extraordinary commitment.

Beyond the emphasis on customer service is an increased emphasis on corporate social responsibility, which also introduces more contingency into executive life. It creates a whole new set of performance criteria that may not fit very naturally with requirements for improved financial performance. Just how to blend these disparate criteria is a matter of ongoing debate and experimentation in hundreds of companies. As deregulation takes hold of the public consciousness in the mid and late nineties, social responsibility itself is becoming an unstable and turbulent idea. What does it mean if it no longer just means complying with government regulations? Deregulation adds to the white water in all organizations.

The pressure for organizational multiculturalism (including internationalizing the corporate culture) and diversity presents another new set of imponderables to leaders and managers. Simply put, what formerly could be taken for granted about what employees are like, due to their relative homogeneity of cultural background, increasingly cannot be taken for granted; and misreadings of cultural expectations and preferences can introduce conflict and resistance into a system where they might never have appeared before.

These are just some of the organizational initiatives now going on that add to the white water for everyone. In general, virtually anything new and different that is tried in an organization will be experienced by significant numbers of members as adding to organizational stress, complexity, and unpredictability.

I am certainly not saying that change is bad nor that organization members are necessarily moved to oppose changes; many changes are in fact *intended* to calm the churning waters a bit, even if this often is not achieved. However, I am saying that given a context of permanent white water, it is almost impossible for any planned change, however well-intentioned, not to contribute further to the turbulence and uncertainty.

Learning as a Response to White Water

Permanent white water puts organizations and their members in the position of continually doing things they have little experience with or have never done before at all. The feeling of "playing a whole new ball game" thoroughly pervades organizational life (Vaill, 1989a, pp. 23–27). *This means that beyond all of the other new skills and attitudes that permanent white water requires, people have to be (or become) extremely effective learners.*

The importance of learning, particularly *lifelong learning*, has been stressed repeatedly over the past two or three decades by educators, political leaders, and social commentators. The validity of these calls to arms is finally being confirmed by our experiences in the permanent white water of modern organizations: we are all playing catch-up; few people feel that they are sufficiently up to date in the knowledge and skills their jobs require, and even those who are superbly prepared are realizing that obsolescence is typically not an abstract idea but a fast-approaching reality. The presence of permanent white water demands that we look anew at the challenge of continual lifelong learning—what it involves, what the barriers are, and whether we even understand it well enough to practice it.

Learning: A Definition

In a variety of ways, this book will make a great deal of the idea of learning. Therefore, at the outset, I offer a definition of *learning*, to serve as a benchmark for the following discussion.

A few moments reflection will reveal that learning is not an easy phenomenon to define for at least two reasons: it is a process not a state, and it occurs as both as overt observable behavior and as an inner condition of attitudes, ideas, and feelings. In short, human learning—particularly *white water learning* for managerial leadership—cannot be discussed in the same terms as the "learning" of a rat in a maze.

Learning obviously often involves acquiring the ability to do something—an ability that we often describe as possessing *know-how*. But in humans, learning has to be more than that. Separately from know-how, we also are able to develop over time a fuller and fuller understanding of a subject in and of itself, even when we do not possess a high degree of its relevant skill component. In other words, we can grow in our *know-what*, whether or not we also grow in our know-how. Beyond know-how and know-what, we can grow in our understanding of the meaning and value of the subject or activity and come to see it in its larger context as a form of human activity. This we can call our *know-why*. We need to understand human learning in terms of all three dimensions: know-how, know-what, and know-why. They are related to each other, but they do not have to move in lockstep: a change in one does not automatically cause a change in the other two.

Accordingly, I define *learning* as follows:

LEARNING: *Changes a person makes in himself or herself that increase the know-why and/or the know-what and/or the know-how the person possesses with respect to a given subject.*

♦   ♦   ♦   ♦   ♦   ♦   ♦

As I have reflected on the learning problems posed by permanent white water, I have come to the conclusion that there are indeed formidable barriers to conducting the kind of continual learning that we need. In the next chapter, two major matters are discussed: first, what some of the fundamental ideas about learning in our culture seem to be; and second, how these ideas may *prevent* us from engaging in white water learning, the kind of learning that permanent white water requires.

Part I

. . . .

Ways of Learning

Doing versus Being

···

Learning as a Means to Doing

Institutional Learning and
the Institutionalized Learner

Go into a big hotel in a large city in the United States (or in fact anywhere in the world) on any given weekday morning, and a stroll down a back corridor on the first floor will take you past room after room set up in classroom style. Outside the rooms are program registration tables piled with name tags and handout materials. Nearby are pitchers of juice, coffee urns, and platters of Danish pastries. Every few yards along the hall are banks of pay telephones, which program participants use at every opportunity. The conference rooms themselves are almost always windowless, filled to designed capacity with chairs and usually tables. At each place is a tablet with the letterhead of either the hotel or the conference convener, along with a pencil or a specially labelled pen. A podium and an overhead projector are stationed front and center. A flipchart poses discreetly to one side, deferring to the prepackaged materials that the speaker usually brings.

If you were to continue your stroll down the hall to the coffee shop, you might see a program presenter, who probably came in late last night, having breakfast with a conference director and one or two staff. They are going over the program objectives, what else the participants have been doing, the schedule for breaks and lunch, which aspects of the presenter's bio will be read to the participants, and a last-minute check on logistics, such as whether the presenter has brought along enough handouts.

Another day of conferences and workshops is about to begin.

If you were taking your stroll in a company or professional train-ing center rather than a hotel, the fixtures and facilities would be more state of the art. Videotape equipment would be increasingly in evidence, and it won't be long before there are computer terminals at each place, no matter what the subject under discussion. Many hotels, too, are adding a separate conference center to the hotel proper, with thoroughly professional state-of-the-art educational facilities. As you observe them, you realize that such conference cen-ters are becoming significant competitive factors, the apparent pre-sumption being that the more high-tech and sumptuous the facilities, the more impact the learning experience will have on potential par-ticipants. Only the corporate training directors know how much this rapid escalation of facilities has added to the cost per participant. One of the first books about these kinds of learning programs was called *Informal Adult Education* (Knowles, 1950). One would hardly term what is going on today in these settings informal!

* * * * * * *

These programs are the postindustrial university. Tens of thousands of men and women experience this environment every day of the year and have been for going on half a century. Those who present material regularly in these settings are the university faculty. Many, maybe most, have Ph.D.s. Many are also professors in traditional colleges and universities. The skills they practice in these new set-tings are not unlike the traditional professor's, although the style is adapted to an adult audience, employing more humor, more breaks, less required prereading, and more frequent references to the "back home situation" than does the traditional classroom style. Some of the content one could find in a college curriculum, but much of it is too specialized, advanced, and/or interdisciplinary to have sur-vived the filters of the average academic curriculum committee.

I have taken a minute to evoke these very familiar learning scenes because I want both to celebrate and to critique them. I think it is both laudable and essential that this level of commitment is being made to lifelong learning. I have myself spent hundreds of hours in these settings, on both sides of the podium. I am convinced that these efforts to continue our learning are our main positive strategy for coping with the extraordinary organizational and societal conditions that I call permanent white water.

We have made an external commitment to lifelong learning in the form of all these millions of hours and training dollars we are investing every day. But what about the inner process of learning? Do we actually know what is being accomplished in all these hours of study and of talk? What do we know about the actual learning processes that are occurring? What do we know about the feelings of the participants? What do *they* think they are doing? What is their image of this activity? Do they experience it as learning? Do they take it seriously? Do they have insights and breakthroughs, and do they experience the commitments to future action that we hope occur as part of an effective learning process?

Certainly their learning is evaluated—these programs employ more intensive evaluations, probably, than the end-of-semester exercises we all routinely completed during our formal schooling. Yet what is being evaluated? Is it the attainment of program-specific knowledge and skills solely, or does it extend to the moods and feelings of participants, to questions of their growth and development as persons, and to increases in their readiness to participate in such programs again? How much serious evaluation do participants do according to their own criteria? How many managers who are going through various workshops put on by their companies or industry groups see themselves developing as learners? How many walk out of an intensive session at the end of the day taking inventory of the things they did well and the things they did not do so well *as learners?* Is anyone encouraging them to think of themselves as developing learners, as learning about learning even as they are absorbing subject matter?

The basic question from which all these other questions derive is what is the philosophy of learning exhibited in these everyday educational and training settings? Once we identify that philosophy, we will want to ask more questions. Is that philosophy adequate to the learning challenges posed by permanent white water? Is there anything essentially wrong here? Is there anything fundamental that we should be viewing differently? I am convinced that the answer to the last question is yes. We need to know a lot more about ourselves and others as learners if all the time and dollars being expended on lifelong learning are to pay off for the individuals and organizations involved in it. We need to know a lot more about learning.

Learning: Some Preliminary Reflections

Learning—the word is all around us, permeating our experiences and our interpretations of situations. We use it in defense ("I've got a lot to learn"), in admiration ("a learned person"), and ruefully ("that was a real learning experience"). We "learn by our mistakes" unless we are "too old to learn," which presumably we never are. For no matter our age, we can "learn by doing" and "live and learn" and are "never too old to learn." Our heroes often had a "love of learning" in their childhoods, or else they "learned the hard way," on the way up. When we say a person finally "learned his lesson," we are speaking of an intensive, painful, disciplining experience.

It is in kindergarten that we first encounter an implicit model of the learning process that remains with us into adulthood. In this chapter, I describe this model that pervades our educational systems and practices, both formally in our schools and in all forms of the training and development for adults that we use to try to keep up with the rapidly changing world we live in. While this model is not absolutely useless for the learning challenges we face, it is inadequate by itself, and in many ways, it is actually dysfunctional for the learning tasks and opportunities facing us. We can begin to form a picture of our existing implicit model by briefly considering three of its implicit principles: that learning is painful, that learning goals are given to us, and that the person setting out to learn is much less admirable than the person who has completed a set amount of learning.

Consider the situation of a learner in our present culture. A learner is by definition a relative beginner; yet it is not a good thing to be a beginner in this culture, especially if one is an adult and especially if cultural norms suggest that one already should know what one is just now starting out to learn. Ours is a culture of achievements and accomplishments. Merit badges abound in many forms, not just on the sleeves of Boy Scouts. To be called an amateur is unfortunately not a compliment; an amateur is "one lacking in experience and competence in an art or science," says *Merriam Webster's Collegiate Dictionary* (10th ed.). That the word derives from the Latin for "lover" is not something that means much to people these days; that indeed there may be something about learning that involves, even requires, *love* of the subject is not a matter we hear discussed very often.

When you undertake a learning process of any kind in our present culture, the object is to move from the state of being a beginner to the state of being an accomplished performer, no matter what the activity is. The most popular word for the goal of learning is "competence." "Mastery" is another term we hear, and there are doubtless many others, all of which refer in some way to getting out of the state of being a beginner. People who remain beginners for too long are dubbed "slow learners," and for the most part, we are unconcerned about the cruelty just beneath the surface in all our kidding of such people. Doubtless each one of us has at one time or another been in such a position or, at least, has striven mightily not to fall into it.

All of these cultural characteristics are exacerbated and the dilemmas of beginners intensified when what is to be learned is "soft," relatively unstructured, and undergoing continual change in the white water; when it is a mixture of new skills, evolving knowledge, unfamiliar attitudes, and perhaps controversial new values. In the previous chapter, I mentioned a number of phrases that we hear all the time in organizations and that reflect people's awareness of permanent white water. The situation of the beginner, particularly the leader who is also a beginner, brings to mind the frequency with which we hear of the "blind leading the blind." While usually intended as a cynical or despairing remark, it is in fact often *existentially true* in the world of permanent white water!

Even though we are uneasy with beginners in our culture, in the 1960s, we began to use the phrase *lifelong learning* to describe our growing intuition that there could and should be no let up in our learning process if we were to live effectively *and comfortably* (!) in a world of increasing challenge and change. What we did not realize, however, was that our ideas about what learning is—its forms, settings, success criteria, and so forth—impede genuine practice of the attitudes and actions that should constitute lifelong learning. Indeed, it is not too much to say that for many of us, lifelong learning describes merely a continuation of the attitudes and actions of our school days, enriched perhaps by nicer facilities and more superficially charming and polished instructors, and made more relevant perhaps by the job challenges that occasion it, but not different in kind from the experiences that began for us in kindergarten and continued for the next sixteen or so years of our lives. This is why the setting sketched at the beginning of this chapter is so familiar and so common: it reflects the debt adult training programs owe to formal school models of the learning process. My task in this chapter is to describe more fully this implicit model of the learning process, this model that is getting in the way of true lifelong learning.

Neither our institutionalized education nor our wider culture has emphasized the possibility and value of a fully developed consciousness of ourselves as learners and of the implicit models of the nature of learning that any educational system embodies. The idea that learning is onerous and painful, basically a struggle, hangs on as a guiding image. We remain hopeful, in any learning project, that we will find a protocol or a magic pill that will relieve us from what we *assume* will be the hard business of going through a learning process. It is in our nature as humans to have constant inner impulses to learn both skills and areas of knowledge. But external demands on us to learn a certain thing in a certain way intrude on these inner impulses so that they are often minimized or apologized for or postponed, sometimes for years, or relegated to the status of "hobbies" and "pastimes."

In a curious and rather tragic way, our learned images of learning prepare us to have a tough time. Our images of learning do not reinforce learning! Learning remains an uphill battle, a strain, an exercise in frustration. No wonder the romance of the phrase "lifelong learning" is hardly matched by our experience. If a person's lifelong learning is to occur productively and reasonably comfortably for the indefinite future (and that is precisely what effective lifelong learning requires), we need to understand our inherited images of the learning process more fully, and we need to consider whether more effective images and models might be available to guide and give meaning to that learning.

Because so much of our conscious experience with learning is in activity that someone else has assigned to us—a parent, a teacher, an employer, someone we're competing against—learning for many of us is a *means to an end that is not of our choosing.* We go through a learning process in pursuit of a goal we have been told is important. As beginners, we are goaded with reasons for beginning, and these reasons are the learning goals that have been given to us.

A variety of names for the broad image of learning and the learning process that I have been describing come to mind. My first impulse was to call this model "learning as a means to being," because learning is seen to be the way that a person becomes qualified, a fully competent person rather than a neophyte, rookie, or beginner. A colleague has suggested that "learning as a means to doing" also fits this model, since learning in our culture is so powerfully oriented to usefulness. Another possible name is "extrinsic model of learning," to capture the idea that both the stimulus for learning and the material to be learned are implicitly assumed to originate outside the learner; they do not depend on the learner for their validity or value. Borrowing from David Riesman's famous distinction (1950), I might call the existing model "other-directed learning," because the learner's attention is so powerfully directed to issues and subject matter as defined by authority figures outside him- or herself. Ivan Illich would doubtless say that what I am talking about is his "Schooling Model" (Illich, 1971). However, the name I have settled upon is institutional learning.

The Prevailing Model: Institutional Learning

Above all, the problem with our existing model of learning is that it depicts learning as an institutional activity. This existing model has been overtaken by the rate of change in organizations and society, just as so many others ideas and practices have been. Permanent white water not only creates extraordinary learning challenges for us all, it also places enormous stress on the theories and forms of learning we practice to meet these challenges. Permanent white water forces us to rethink the collection of ideas about learning that has been shaped by our tradition of acquiring our knowledge in formal settings and that I therefore call *institutional learning*.

Institutional here carries two senses: first, I use it to mean being thoroughly *institutionalized* in philosophy and practice and thoroughly paradigmatic, being a self-renewing system of ideas that is not under anyone's control nor derives from any single source. Second, I use it in what might be called the "bricks and mortar" sense to signify the identification of learning with educational systems embodied in buildings and in formal organizations ranging from kindergartens through graduate schools and more recently on into the major institutions of adult education and training that exist both inside companies and other organizations and as free-standing institutions.

Institutional learning is a set of ideas that can be found everywhere in the developed world. These ideas are not without merit, and it is not the intention of this book to create a new model that denies the prevailing one. It is also not my intent needlessly to bash the model of learning that is pervasively practiced in our formal educational and training settings. There are plenty of learning tasks for which this model is perfectly adequate, but for the most part, they are not the same learning tasks that arise in permanent white water. Therefore, we need some new ways of thinking about learning if we are to meet our new challenges.

In the next few paragraphs, I delineate the model of institutional learning by spelling out the assumptions it makes about the learning process. These assumptions have functioned as our criteria for what constitutes good learning. When these assumptions are fulfilled, our further assumption has been that effective learning will occur. As noted previously, few of us ever received much encouragement to develop our own criteria for effective learning. Instead, we unconsciously learned to associate certain given criteria with learning. When we adhered to these criteria, we were constantly encouraged to think that "good learning" was occurring, and when we did not adhere to them, that our learning was occurring "improperly" or not at all.

Good Learning in the Institutional Learning Model

In what follows, I discuss the implicit criteria for good learning in the institutional learning model rather uncritically, since, as I have mentioned, they are valid for some learning conditions. However, it should be understood that *permanent white water questions or flatly invalidates most of them*. Under white water conditions, the assumptions the model makes often do not hold. Permanent white water requires a different set of ideas about what good learning is (these ideas are presented in Chapter Two).

The institutional learning philosophy can be found everywhere. It is seen in most training and development experiences in the work world. It runs all through colleges and universities. It occurs in adult education undertaken voluntarily. It is present when we learn sports, hobbies, and other recreational activities. We carry the model with us everywhere whether we are the learners (a term I use throughout to cover all kinds of learners, not just young people in school), or the instructors, coaches, or mentors.

The essence of the philosophy of institutional learning is its goal directedness: learning is assumed to depend on the *learner's desire to achieve some specific goal*, usually defined as possessing new knowledge or some skill that was not possessed before the learning began. In addition to goal directedness, the model contains three other fundamental assumptions. First, both the goal to be achieved and the material relevant to achieving it are assumed capable of clear specification. Obviously, for learning to be goal directed, it must be possible to state the goal clearly enough so that a learner can comprehend it and, at least to some degree, connect the goal to the learning behaviors that are required of him or her. As a result, institutional learning encourages a learner to expect and an instructor to provide as much clear relevance for the material to be learned as possible. Implicitly, the belief is that the learner's time should not be wasted with peripheral matters.

The second assumption deriving from goal directedness is that the *learner will value the goal* toward which the learning is directed, including any interim or surrogate rewards (for example, grades, praise, and the like) that are intended to keep the learner on the path to the goal. Institutional learning's effectiveness depends on the learner's valuing the rewards that are available and wanting to please those who control these rewards. Related to this is the philosophy's assumption that though they may not be the methods of first choice, fear and punishment are justifiable means to get learners to value the goals of learning and the actions that need to be taken to reach those goals. In this model, learners ought to want to learn. Learning is a moral duty. Therefore, a learner who does not understand this imperative must be persuaded. Of course, what the institutional learning model ultimately assumes is not just that learners ought to want to learn but also, and more importantly, that *they ought to want to reach the goals that their parents, teachers, train-ers, coaches, mentors, and/or supervisors have decided are the important ones.* It is not learning per se that fear and punishment focus on; it is to ensure the learner's adoption of these external goals that fear and punishment are used.

Third, *the learning goal is assumed to be outside the learning process.* It is not expected that the content, the meaning, or the value of the goal will be contingent on the learning process itself. Instead, the goal is assumed to be a fixed element in the overall process; it does not lie in the beholder's eye. The learner and the specific actions taken to reach the goal are the variables, not the goal itself.

Once the learner understands, accepts, and values the goals of the institutional learning process, another assumption immediately appears, namely, that the *efficiency of the learning process* is a matter of prime concern. Given that the goal has been clearly specified and the relevant material to be learned clearly identified, institutional learning holds that it should be possible to determine the best way for learning to proceed.

Speed of learning is an outgrowth of efficiency of learning and thus yet another assumption running through the model's ideas for a good learning process. The faster the learner can go (without sac-rificing "comprehension"), the better. Generations of learners have felt this criterion pressing on them as the books to be read piled up on the windowsill, as the wall clock in an exam room raced around, or as an "all-nighter" dissolved into dawn and the deadline for brief-ing the big boss loomed. That the *volume of material covered* is important is another spinoff assumption from the general concern with efficiency. This volume is taken to equate with the amount that must have been learned. The more books read and references consulted, the more courses taken, the more credits earned, the more years invested in a learning process, the more books one has on the shelf and databases one has accessed, the greater the learning that has occurred. Sacrifices of time and money on behalf of learn-ing punctuate these efficiency, speed, and volume criteria: stories abound of men and women who earned an advanced degree at night, or crammed for the CPA exam, or absorbed all the implications of a new piece of legislation in a weekend . . . while holding down a full-time job and raising a family . . . and training for their first marathon.

Combine the criteria of efficiency, speed, and volume with the three philosophical principles of goal directedness, learners' responsibility to value the goals, and learners' lack of responsibility for originating goals, and you have the main ingredients of the institutional learning model. It is a powerful framework, indeed a dazzling one. It developed back in the nineteenth century and has become deeply implanted in all cultures that value education and training for both their young people and their workforces.

One clear implication of all this model's characteristics is that *institutional learning is likely to be answer oriented,* and indeed, it has ingrained generations of learners with an obsession with getting the "right answer." This is how the learner knows that he or she has reached the learning goal: a correct answer is attained as a result of manipulating tools or data or ideas the "proper" way, the way that has been taught. Getting the right answer is one of the institutional learner's most reliable indices that learning has occurred.

It is well, also, to consider how our *learning culture* has grown up as a reflection of institutional learning. At a recent conference on executive development, a senior executive described his company's bold new commitment to executive education. The centerpiece of his evidence was a slide showing the company's new auditorium built for executive training. Plush seats were arrayed row on row in a traditional theater style. A large stage in the front of the hall featured an impressive lectern carefully positioned. The entire scene was a perfect embodiment of the instructional assumptions of the institutional learning model, as are the classroom settings of hotel-based training programs. Other institutional learning features of training programs are that program participants are assumed to be *qualified* to be there (for example, if the program covers "advanced" material, they are assumed to have completed the necessary "basic" work). If there is "prereading" (the adult education euphemism for homework), they are expected to have done it. Behind these ideas lies the assumption that *learning is cumulative*: it is to be designed and delivered in a cumulative style, and it is, supposedly, cumulatively stored in the cortex. The assumed cumulative nature of learning also supports the assumption just mentioned that there are basic and advanced levels in any subject and a learner cannot start at the advanced level without having completed the "prerequisites." (That "pre" in "prerequisite" is literally superfluous, by the way, but the repetition it provokes intensifies the word's meaning and, in this context, makes more emphatic the notion that the learner is supposed to have somehow prepared beforehand. It pays to *listen* to and dissect the vocabulary that has grown up to support institutional learning philosophy.)

The whole physical design of formal learning environments communicates to the learner that "the people who set up this room and this program know what you need to learn; your job is to learn it." It is not expected that learners and their instructor will, for example, rearrange all the chairs and tables to support a different way of learning. Of course, that does happen, but the assumption is that it will not happen and, most importantly, that there is no reason for it to happen.

The implicit messages stored physically in the learning environment are examples of another general feature of the institutional learning model—*learners are expected to follow the rules.* Teachers, trainers, and consultants often decry learners' desires for a "cookbook" or a "five-point checklist," but that obsession is understandable when you look at the cues that surround learning settings. There is very little that communicates to the learner, "You are expected to take coresponsibility for the basic design of this learning effort." Instead, most of the cues say, "You are to make good use of what has been placed in this learning setting for you."

The setting also communicates to the learner in another important sense. In response to the learner's unspoken question, "Do I have any friends, supporters, soul mates, co-learners here?" the setting replies, "You're on your own." Of course, people *do* look around the room and notice friends and supporters, but the institutional learning philosophy does not attach much importance to this. It does not anticipate that learners will be looking around the room and undertake to help them "locate" themselves in relation to the others present. Even when there are name tags or a roster of attendees, and even when the group is small enough that brief introductions are undertaken, these gestures are perfunctory—"hygiene factors" as Frederick Herzberg might call them (1959). Such practices are assumed to be extraneous to learning. It is unlikely that a program leader following the institutional learning model would open a session for corporate executives by saying, "Let's see who's here and what your expectations and learning preferences are. Based on that, we can take this program today in any of a number of directions." It is not that such statements never get made, but rather that institutional learning does not encourage such invitations, increasingly presenters are not making them, and learners themselves seem to consider them somewhat peripheral to the main reason everyone is in the room, which is to learn "the material."

So we have a combination of powerful messages to follow the rules, a strong hint that the presence of friends and supporters is not of any crucial importance, and learning material that is itself new. This combination leaves the learner in a disempowered state. It is not that institutional learning is consciously oppressive. It does not assume that the learner should be maliciously humbled and demeaned. It is just that institutional learning assumes that *learning begins in confusion and involves considerable inconvenience and pain* before it moves to a state of relative competence and comfort. Beginning learners are seen as "rookies," "neophytes," "plebes," "new kids on the block," "just getting started," "wet behind the ears," "looking for a security blanket," "wandering around in a daze," "still getting acclimated"—the condescending phrases for the disempowered learner spring readily to mind. It is a good deal harder to think of common phrases that honor the beginner and portray that person as captain of his or her own "learning ship."

The learner's life under institutional learning can thus be lonely. Learning is assumed to be a *relatively private process* that goes on "off-line" from the places where the fruits of learning are to be used—the workplace or the family, for example. Moreover, it is up to the expert-instructor to decide when learning has occurred and can be certified. The loneliness is compounded for many learners when competition is introduced, whether in school, at one's place of work, or in recreational activities. Institutional learning assumes that competition among learners is good for learning.

It is not surprising that learners come to feel inferior, at least relative to those who have more "learning" on a subject than they do. And the model is thoroughgoing. Since it is adhered to in virtually all learning projects at all levels of society, there is a basic psychological state one enters as a learner—a state of felt inferiority; of tentativeness, cautiousness, and dependence on those in authority; and of suppression of here-and-now feelings in favor of anticipations of future comfort and success. These characteristics describe a person with a substantially diminished sense of self, a person who is not yet an authentic being but who is going to try to learn as the means to becoming an authentic being, a real person.

Under these conditions, learners act out their "lost" state in a number of ways. Some become hostile and openly resist. They usually cannot give a very complete account of what is bothering them, but what they can say expresses their hatred of their disempowered state. Some learners become depressed; some become accident-prone and manifest other physical stress symptoms. Some retreat into a kind of faceless sociability, becoming one of the gang and always ready to go along with what's happening.

Perhaps most unfortunately of all, given today's need for learning strategies for permanent white water, some of the brightest and most energetic learners become superachievers within the criteria and assumptions of institutional learning. They read and remember more, and they do it faster. They orient their attention toward those who possess the expert knowledge and are not distracted by the learners who are not as comfortable. Some of these superachievers are largely free of negative fantasies about the system and do not fight it openly. They may exhibit creativity, sometimes of very high quality but almost always *within* the goals and objectives that are defined by the instructor and/or the traditions surrounding the subject matter. These high achievers who have accepted the institutional learning parameters are almost never outrageous or revolutionary in their work, either in the way that they perform it or in its results.

Such high-performing individuals are often fearful and obsessive about their performance in any learning situation. Institutional learning philosophy so thoroughly dominates their thinking that if they are not succeeding by the standards of the system, they become very nervous and manifest considerable stress. Everyone has felt this anxiety to some degree—the fear that one won't "get" what one is supposed to. The fear can be extreme in some cases, leading to extraordinary feats of intense studying, but this is what the model says one is *supposed* to be doing—suffering.

There is of course no reason why learning should entail an instructor's inflicting pain on a learner. People can learn without pain. It is institutional learning philosophy that is principally responsible for the belief. At bottom, *institutional learning is as much a system for indoctrination and control as it is a system for learning.* Indeed, the philosophy may only nominally be about learning for its own sake. To a much greater degree, it is about learning on very special terms. It is about learning predefined material. It is about learning from someone in an authoritative position relative to the learner, about something that is already known. It is about learning as a member of a group—or "cohort" as some call it—a group in which everyone is supposed to learn pretty much the same thing. It is about learning that must go on at a preset pace, in a preset physical space, with preset materials to be studied, and preset performance standards to be met. *Of course* learning under these conditions is going to be painful, with even the most compliant and the most successful learners feeling resentment at the regimentation that is built into it.

Permanent White Water as a Challenge to Institutional Learning

The permanent white water in today's systems is creating a situation in which institutional learning patterns are simply inadequate to the challenge. Subject matter is changing too fast. Learners' demographics are changing too rapidly. Learners are interweaving their learning with work responsibilities and expecting their learning to be directly relevant to these responsibilities. Traditional instructor roles are dissolving, and other, more informal mentor roles are arising. Technology is delivering materials to learners in lots of ways other than face-to-face meetings with expert-instructors in a classroom setting. The formal educational institutions that play such a large role in sustaining the institutional learning philosophy are themselves feeling the white water in their budgets, in their labor relations, in the strident demands of their various stakeholders, in their crumbling physical plants, and in their difficulties in finding competent leadership.

Neither the philosophy nor practice of institutional learning was designed for permanent white water—neither in formal educational systems themselves nor in the worlds that learners enter as "graduates" of those educational systems. As a result, our thinking about learning is in a period of extraordinary ferment. The problem is to envision what learning can be, how it can go on given that the traditional paradigm for conducting it is not designed for the task and is in many ways inadequate under contemporary conditions. We have to learn what learning in permanent white water can be.

Permanent white water events are (as I described in the Introduction) novel, messy surprises that require immediate action and that are going to continue presenting themselves to us indefinitely. Typically, there is no relevant body of information and few identifiable skills that can be quickly activated to solve the problem or contain the crisis.

It has been noted many times in recent decades that learning must go on continually in our macrosystem environments. Learning must be a way of being—an ongoing set of attitudes and actions by individuals and groups that they employ to try to keep abreast of the surprising, novel, messy, obtrusive, recurring events thrown up by these macrosystems. At the least, learning as a way of being must supplement institutional learning. In many situations, learning as a way of being must supplant institutional learning as the fundamental philosophy and practice of human learning.

Learning as a Way of Being: An Introduction

What is learning as a way of being, aside from a memorable phrase? It is the task of the rest of this book to show that learning as a way of being has real substance, that it is an authentic way of living and working, thinking and feeling, in the world of permanent white water.

What would learning be like in permanent white water? That is this book's fundamental question. And where in the world can we safely say a person does *not* have white water learning challenges and opportunities? I have chosen to write mainly about the world of work, but are we going to say that family life is exempt from white water? Recreational life? Devotional and spiritual life? Life as a citizen of a community and nation? Life as a participant in various voluntary groups? Life as a sports fan or participant? Retirement life? And indeed, in an age of Kevorkianian complexities, what Brodkey calls "the life that is dying itself" (Brodkey, 1994, p. 84)?

Since turbulent conditions appear everywhere and pervade our lives in both time and space, learning in permanent white water conditions is and will continue to be a constant way of life for all of us—thus the phrase *learning as a way of being*.[1] Learning in permanent white water *is* learning as a way of being. That equation is my basic point of departure. As noted in the Introduction, permanent white water is not just a collection of facts and events external to us. It is *felt*—as confusion and loss of direction and control, as a gnawing sense of meaninglessness. If learning is to be a major means of restoring our understanding of the world around us, the learning process itself should not *add* to our feeling of meaninglessness. Yet this is precisely what the institutional learning model tends to do as it renders the learner passive and dependent, inundates the learner with great volumes of miscellaneous subject matter presented as absolutely essential knowledge, and then erects a powerful set of extrinsic rewards and punishments to keep the learner's focus on all this jumbled and largely meaningless content. By inadvertently creating meaningless learning experiences, institutional learning exacerbates white water problems and leaves the learner unsure of how he or she is ever going to live effectively in the chaotic organizations of the present and future.

In the phrase learning as a way of being, *being* refers to the whole person—to something that goes on all the time and that extends into all aspects of a person's life; it means all our levels of awareness and, indeed, must include our unconscious minds. If learning as a way of being is a mode for everyone, being then must include interpersonal being as well as personal socially expressive being—my learning as a way of being will somehow exist in relation to your learning as a way of being. In short, there are no boundaries to being. There is not something about a human of which we would say, "This is not part of human being." Clearly, learning as a way of being is a very capacious idea.

---

1. Hall has said, "Man, the animal with the most highly evolved brain, is above all a learning organism. He is designed to learn. The only questions are: How does he do it? And under what circumstances and settings does he do it best?" (1977, p. 173). Thus, I could speak of learning as *the* way to be, rather than as *a* way of being. However, learning as a way of being teaches us other ways of being, and so I have chosen to use the phrase that acknowledges the possibility of other ways of being.

Learning as a way of being probably encompasses a somewhat different set of attitudes and behaviors for each person, considering our differences in experience, beliefs and values (including cultural norms and taboos), kinds and levels of intelligence, and learning styles (Kolb, 1984). It is not an objective phenomenon with identical manifestations. The phenomenon appears in every person since it is part of the essence of being human, but each individual uniquely experiences and expresses it. Nevertheless, my basic contention remains: learning as a way of being is a natural mode of being that is more important than ever in a complex and unstable environment, but it has been profoundly suppressed and distorted by the highly structured learning practices of institutional learning.

Even though each of us will live out learning as a way of being in a different way, our common experience with institutional learning suggests that for each of us there will be some common challenges as we develop our mode of learning as a way of being. Below, I list seven qualities, or modes, of learning as a way of being (LWB) that meet two criteria: first, they tend to be absent entirely from institutional learning or at least tightly controlled by its philosophy and practice; and second, they are kinds of learning that appear to be especially important in the world of permanent white water. Doubtless these are not the only learning challenges that are posed by white water. Further development of the idea of learning as a way of being, as well as its specific use by any given person, will uncover others. But these seven will more than do for the moment, as each of us considers what learning as a way of being might be like for himself or herself.

Self-Directed Learning (LWB1)

Permanent white water frequently poses learning challenges for which no textbooks or other learning materials have been specifically designed. Indeed, a learner in white water may be the *only* person, so far as he or she knows, who has a particular learning need. Therefore, effective learning in permanent white water has to be marked by a high degree of self-direction. (Conversely, the institutional learning model prestructures learning for the learner and thus does not foster either the attitudes or abilities of self-directed learning.)

Creative Learning (LWB2)

Permanent white water continually poses novel learning problems in which it is not clear what exactly has to be learned or what the learning will look like when, as, and if it is acquired. Though not often remarked upon, what we call creativity is a mode of learning in which the creator is not pursuing a preset goal using preset methods and resources. Creativity is exploration; to be an explorer is literally not to know exactly where you are going—that is the essence of exploration. Learning in permanent white water has to be strongly creative, exploratory, and inventive. (Conversely, the institutional learning model pays lip service to encouraging creativity but keeps control of just when, where, and how much creativity the learner will be permitted and stresses learning as the taking in of other people's ideas. As a result, institutional learning learners are not well prepared for the creative learning that permanent white water requires.)

Expressive Learning (LWB3)

We all know the mode of learning described in the metaphor of learning to swim by being pushed off the dock. Much learning in permanent white water has this quality: the learning occurs in the process of expressing it (in contrast to the more orderly institutional learning mode in which something is first learned in an off-line environment and then expressed or performed). Permanent white water often does not permit the luxury of off-line learning. Learners need to be comfortable with learning as they go along.

Feeling Learning (LWB4)

Permanent white water poses upsetting learning problems. It can make the learner feel stupid; it can cause confusion and fear. Trying to learn in an environment of constant unpredictable change can lead learners to feel that they are not getting anywhere—or indeed are going backward, becoming progressively *more* incompetent. Learning in white water, therefore, occurs as much at the level of one's feelings as it does at the level of ideas and skills. It has to be learning about *meanings*—how meanings are formed, how they are challenged or lost, how they can be sustained and revitalized. To know the *meaning* of something is not just to have impersonal ideas about it but to know it deeply and personally. (The institutional learning model, however, tends to ignore learning meanings that involve deep feelings, again failing to prepare learners for learning in permanent white water.)

On-Line Learning (LWB5)

All environments are learning environments for the human being, especially the person who is spending large amounts of time in work environments of constant change. Thus, learning as a way of being is deinstitutionalized learning. Metaphorically speaking, it is on-line learning (in diametrical opposition to off-line institutional learning).

Continual Learning (LWB6)

Learning as a way of being requires that we think through what it means to be learning throughout our lives. "Lifelong learning," now a virtual cliché, needs to be reclaimed from that status so we can see what it means for a learner's life. By forcing a continuing stream of novel learning problems on the learner, permanent white water keeps the learner feeling like a beginner (a psychological condition that the institutional learning model trains learners to avoid and denigrate). Personal mastery in permanent white water is almost a contradiction in terms (although it is the institutional learning model's ideal). Thus, we need to think further about how continual learning can be done in a healthy way.

Reflexive Learning (LWB7)

The previous six modes of learning are very difficult, especially when the philosophy of institutional learning takes at best an equivocal position on them and often actively discourages them. Thus, learning as a way of being has to include learning about learning itself. The practice of learning as a way of being is a process of becoming a more conscious and reflective learner, more aware of one's own learning process and how it compares to the learning processes of others. (Conversely, institutional learning depends for its power and influence largely on the learner's not engaging in conscious, reflective learning!)

Those Who Thrive on Institutional Learning: A Note

There is one last thing to note about institutional learning philosophy—something that every teacher knows and has perhaps thought of in protest as I have recited one institutional learning flaw after another. Certain kinds of learners thrive in the institutional learning environment. They do not become beaten down, distracted, fearful learners who are just trying to figure out how to please the teacher and escape from the class with a passing grade. They do not act out their frustrations with disruptive behavior or depressive withdrawal or desperate pleas for structure. Instead they learn great globs of information and acquire exciting new abilities and thoroughly enjoy themselves in the process. They go beyond what is required, exhibit creativity and insight, make the subject "their own" in an astonishing variety of ways. They are every teacher's delight, and the occasional appearance of such a student, many a teacher will say, is what keeps him or her in the profession.

How have these exemplary learners acquired the ability to make institutional learning work for them rather than against them? No doubt the answer is the usual complex mixture of nature and nurture and is more properly left to educational and developmental psychology. Nevertheless, one point that can be made here is that these learners engage in learning as a way of being. They enter a learning mode smoothly, across a wide variety of subjects and conditions. Their actions and attitudes continually display various mixes of the seven dimensions of learning as a way of being. Indeed, one source of these seven dimensions has been my own observation of such high-performing learners, and in the next chapter, a good deal more will be made of the way such learners operate. They have been able to hang onto, celebrate, and nurture learning as a way of being within the institutional learning framework, even though that framework discourages learning as a way of being.

One thing they teach us is ironic: institutional learning works best when a learner practices learning as a way of being. This makes the understanding of learning as a way of being all the more important. Institutional learning is suspicious of learning as a way of being and successfully suppresses it in many learners, but that suppression so stultifies the learner and hamstrings learning ability that he or she cannot acquire the good things that institutional learning does have to offer. Institutional learning by itself, that is, in the absence of a learner who embodies learning as a way of being, is thus a self-defeating approach to human learning.

Conclusion

This chapter has presented and critiqued the philosophy of institutional learning, the familiar educational system that virtually all people have been exposed to throughout their lives, first in formal school systems and later in many other settings that (whether deliberately or not) follow the classroom template. Many of the criticisms, both direct and implied, have been and are being made by others. The particular point I make that is not found in other critiques is that institutional learning tends to disqualify us for the kinds of learning we need to do throughout our lives under the conditions of rapid, chaotic change that form our permanent white water. Without our rethinking the institutional learning model, the lifelong learning we all agree is so important will not be what it can be: it will not help people live purposefully and decently under conditions of constant change.

Many readers of this book are probably interested in learning as it goes on in schools and in work organizations, and are probably responsible for formulating policies and managing education and training systems. Understandably, such readers are looking for ways to do a better job of fostering the learning of others in their organizations. In the longer run, this book should help such readers meet that objective. However, in the shorter run, readers are asked to suspend temporarily the question of how to implement learning as a way of being. If my thesis is correct, our habits acquired from institutional learning will tempt us to think of learning as a way of being pedantically, as a "subject" or a "learning theory" to be "applied" to learning problems. That is not what learning as a way of being is. It is a different mentality about *all* learning—formal classroom learning as well as learning from everyday experience. Our first task, then, is to think about learning as a way of being as it can be in ourselves—what it means for us, how we already practice it, and how we might practice it more thoroughly.

A certain righteous anger is not out of place as we consider learning as a way of being. It is, after all, *our* learning that this book is about—yours and mine and that of everyone we know. Why has institutional learning taken so much self-direction and creativity and expressive opportunity out of *our* learning? Why is so little attention paid to *our* feelings as learners? In comparison with *our* work, play, and family life, why should the classroom be the learning environment par excellence? Why has institutional learning not prepared *us* better for lifelong learning, except to teach us to regard it as "continuing our schooling"? Why has it taught *us* so little about ourselves as learners and about the variety of learning experiences available to us in this incredibly rich and varied modern world?

* * * * * * *

In the coming pages, the question is both what does learning as a way of being look like and how can we recover it. The remaining chapters develop the idea of learning as a way of being further, celebrate it, try to strengthen our commitment to it, muse about it and play with it, and even encourage us to dream about what our own learning is like out of its institutional learning straightjacket. Then we will be better able to think about how our own learning as a way of being might be passed on to others, not as structured knowledge and designed learning experiences but as a mood that can color and enrich all learning in whatever form.

2

Learning as a Way of Being

All Experience Is Learning

Learning as a way of being is a whole mentality. It is a way of being in the world. Although I have listed seven modes of it, they are twists of the learning kaleidoscope. They should not be thought of as having independent existence or as items that we can work on one at a time. More than just a skill, learning as a way of being is a whole posture toward experience, a way of framing or interpreting all experience as a learning opportunity or learning process. "Why must anyone seek for new ways of acting?" asked the biologist J. Z. Young. "The answer is that in the long run the continuity of life itself depends on the making of new experiments. . . . [T]he continuous invention of new ways of observing is man's special secret of living" (1960, pp. 65–66).

A phenomenon that thoroughly pervades our way of being and yet is also idiosyncratic and subjective to each individual is difficult to conceive of clearly enough that we can begin to experiment with it for ourselves. My argument has arrived at the idea of learning as a way of being out of the twin realizations of how much permanent white water asks of us as learners and how ill-suited the philosophy of institutional learning is to white water conditions. Learning as a way of being is an inference or hypothesis, therefore. Maybe it won't stand up; maybe it is just romantic nonsense to try to envision a much more versatile and higher-quality mode of learning than institutional learning has developed in us. That is a possibility, but my faith, and I hope yours, is on the other side; it is that enough can be said about learning as a way of being to outline its developmental potential and to help us see how we can begin to practice more thoroughly this philosophy of personal learning.

Another preliminary observation is in order. Today, the world of education and training for managerial leaders[1] is heavily occupied with ideas about learning under the separate but related rubrics of organizational learning and the learning organization. On the one hand, *organizational learning* is learning that goes on inside an organization, usually the learning of an individual but also the learning of pairs or teams of people. The organizational learning movement is thus occupied with questions of the nature of learning in organizational environments and with what managerial leaders can do to enhance learning processes within organizations. The great contribution of this movement is to see the managerial leader as affecting the kind of learning that goes on in an organization and to define one of his or her role responsibilities as enhancing the learning of others. It is only regrettable that the insight that the manager is also a teacher, mentor, and coach and a leader and facilitator of learning has taken so long to become a central postulate of management and leadership theory.

The *learning organization*, on the other hand, is certainly a place where high-quality human learning goes on. But a lot more than this is being signaled by the switching of noun and adjective. The learning organization is a different kind of social system than that envisioned by the dominant concept of organizational theory (with a few landmark exceptions such as Argyris and Schön, 1978, and Weick, 1979). The learning organization is not grudgingly and creakily lurching from one stable state to the next as the world

1. An explanation is in order about the term *managerial leader*. Neither "leader" nor "manager" alone captures the role of the person I have primarily in mind. "Managerial" is necessary because the discussion primarily talks about organizations and the world of work. "Leader" is necessary because today's managers are trying to lead change processes at individual, group, and organizational levels. They are not just "managing" the system.

around it changes. Because it is constantly learning, it is "beyond the stable state" permanently (Schön, 1973). The learning organization in contemporary vision has achieved a new kind of internal structure and process marked by imaginative flexibility of style in its leadership and by empowered contributions from its membership. It is constituted to learn and grow and change—as opposed to traditional bureaucratic models constituted to be stable and predictable in their operation, to hold the line and not to change.

One obvious characteristic of the learning organization, of course, is that it takes human beings—us—to refashion organizational structures and processes in order to achieve learning organizations. We have learning to do if we are to lead or participate in this refashioning. The dynamics of learning organizations depend on new behavior by their members and their constituents. I come back, therefore, to the relative health of our learning abilities and to our understanding of the kinds and degrees of learning that lead the evolution toward learning organizations.

Learning as a way of being is not the same thing as either organizational learning or the learning organization. Rather, it is a companion philosophy, at the personal level, to these and other developments involving learning by managerial leaders and by organizations. In the previous chapter, I said that engaging in learning as a way of being is the key to successful institutional learning. Here, I suggest that it is clearly both a basic form of high-quality organizational learning and a prerequisite attribute of men and women who are to lead the way to the new learning organizations. Learning as a way of being is foundational to all efforts to enhance the learning of managerial leaders.

Finally, there is another way in which learning as a way of being is of central importance to managerial leaders. Today's management literature is packed with exciting statements about the new kinds of things the managerial leader of today and tomorrow needs to be able to do. Amid all these ringing calls to arms—and they are an impressive array of qualities and abilities, and probably quite valid—we may quietly ask, "And how is it that a managerial leader immersed in permanent white water is going to develop these sterling capabilities?" That is the question of the decade, perhaps of the next quarter century. Many of us who are educators have been trying to answer this question with institutional learning, that is, we have been trying to design learning experiences *for* these managerial learners, experiences that will foster the abilities so many thinkers are saying they need. There is a good possibility, though, that we have stumbled onto the limits of institutional learning philosophy and practice in these attempts. Certainly there are hundreds of corporate directors of executive development and many, many M.B.A. program directors who are wondering if their curricula are actually developing the needed qualities in participants. Thinking long range, thinking strategically, handling multiple ambiguous variables at once, staying clear on fundamental vision and values, exuding integrity and steadfastness and interpersonal sensitivity in all one's affairs, handling stress with relative ease—these are abilities that we are no longer sure can be developed in a three-day corporate retreat for "high potentials" or the introductory M.B.A. course in "management and organization." If the truth be told, we are not exactly sure how these qualities develop, although it is a nontrivial observation that they are qualities of character as much as they are behavioral skills, a realization that led me a few years ago to suggest that "executive development is spiritual development" (Vaill, 1990).

One contention of the present book is that we may be looking in the wrong place: we have been looking to institutional learning to provide us with the educational and training experiences needed for managerial leadership. I propose that instead, we develop our thinking about learning as a way of being, about how a managerial leader might begin to practice a way of being himself or herself and thus develop over time the kinds of qualities that life in his or her position requires. This means I have not written this book to teach the reader how to design learning experiences for someone else— even though many readers will have that as one of their own learning objectives. Instead, my aim is to help each reader think about how learning can more fully become his or her way of being.

Thinking and Writing Holistically

For all its significance, *learning as a way of being* is a rather prosaic phrase for the key concept of this book, but the phrase was deliberately chosen. One of the characteristics of the contemporary education and training world is a proliferation of catchy acronyms and labels that supposedly lend weight and credence to the newest learning technique or theory. Learning as a way of being is not necessarily a catchy label, and this is consistent with the descriptive problem that learning as a way of being poses. If we are trying to envision a learning process that is more personal, more present, and more continual than institutional learning, we should try to talk about it in a way that is as true as possible to the way that it operates. A learning process that is a way of being may be many things, but one thing it probably is not is a static list of verbal characteristics that can be summed up in brief labels. Therefore, the following discussion has not been organized to produce a definitive list. Rather, through a process of imaginative reflection, I try to *grow* an understanding of learning as a way of being. I intend the reader to participate in this process, amplifying, modifying, and taking exception as the discussion proceeds, for it is learning as a way of being for all of us that this chapter is talking about.

If along the way in this imaginative process, you find yourself asking, "But after all, what exactly *is* learning as a way of being, and how exactly does it *work?*" recognize that the question is rooted in the distortions institutional learning has introduced into our understanding. That question asks for a definitive, static answer about something—learning—that does not exist as a definitive, static phenomenon. This does not mean, of course, that a discussion of learning as a way of being should not be measured by such criteria as interest, relevance, creativity, and zing. Any model that competes with traditional approaches should have such qualities. It is not a fixed alternative to traditional approaches that we need to fashion though, but a range of possibilities that flows from viewing learning as taking place at the core of our being.

Qualities of Learning as a Way of Being

In the previous chapter, I introduced seven qualities, or modes, of learning as a way of being, which do not define learning as a way of being, since it is not a list, but that are especially important for learning in permanent white water. These seven are

Self-directed learning

Creative learning

Expressive learning

Feeling learning

On-line learning

Continual learning

Reflexive learning

These seven qualities may be thought of as the individual notes out of which learning as a way of being becomes a variety of chords and intricate melodies. I will try to portray them working together—to play the music as it were. (Because this book is mainly concerned with learning for managerial leadership, the music is about that kind of learning.)

The challenge is to envision learning as a way of being, to imagine how these seven notes can interweave and enrich each other in our learning and in the learning of managerial leaders. Each of the seven signals a kind of emphasis or a flavor to learning that is very important and in danger of getting lost in white water, but it would be untrue to the phenomenon of learning as a way of being merely to talk about the seven one at a time and hope that somehow the reader will be able to synthesize them all into a meaningful whole.

It is, in fact, *very hard* to envision learning as a way of being. There is much criticism of institutional learning philosophy in this book, but one can sympathize with it as a solution to many problems that arise in learning situations. It is just so much easier and cleaner to conduct a learning process without much reference to the seven qualities. Think of the logistical problems, for example, of encouraging on-line learning about managerial leadership on the part of the hundred thousand or so students enrolled in M.B.A. programs in the United States. Every one of the seven modes similarly challenges the learner and anyone who would help the learner, and the interweaving of the seven so that they enrich each other increases the challenge exponentially. Because our institutional learning has discouraged such interweaving, we must learn it as we do it, in a learning-as-a-way-of-being process. This interweaving calls for our incorporating all seven of the qualities of learning as a way of being, which is why I have said we have to attend to our own learning first, before we create for others the learning systems and experiences that we hope will correct for institutional learning rigidities. Given these challenges, it would be far too much trouble for us to develop a vision of learning as a way of being were it not for the fact that the world of permanent white water requires it. Learning has to go on in that world, and it has to be learning that interweaves the seven qualities. We do not really have a choice.

In the next few pages, a strategy of accumulation is employed to grow the reader's understanding of what learning as a way of being can be in the world of the managerial leader. After the examination of self-directed learning, discussion of each succeeding quality builds on what has been said about the previous qualities so that the discussion of reflexive learning, the seventh quality, properly shows that quality interacting with the previous six qualities.

Self-Directed Learning (LWB1)

The most fundamental characteristic of learning as a way of being is that it needs to be self-directed. For a variety of reasons, learners in white water have to be largely self-directed learners. First of all, the turbulence of a part of a macrosystem is turbulence *for a particular learner*. It may not feel turbulent to others, and hence there may be no one else who appreciates what needs to be learned to cope with the situation. We know this as personal experience, from our own need to engage in some key piece of learning in the midst of many distractions and competing pressures: for example, when we face tight deadlines with no one else seeming to realize how under-the-gun we feel. Another way to say this is that learning needs and goals can often be unique to a particular learner. Or members of a unique group may need to learn together in order to cope with a particular set of chaotic conditions. This group may have to be self-organizing in the first instance and able to direct for itself the learning process needed (Manz and Sims, 1993). Also, white water events, being novel, often require an imaginative definition of what is to be learned; new kinds of information and modes of knowing may be needed that are not available in the standard courses and other learning packages produced according to institutional learning model. Moreover, even if predesigned learning modules are available, they are often not available when the learner needs them: white water events are not noted for permitting a leisurely sooner-or-later-we'll-get-around-to-it attitude.

There are two basic ideas to be stated about self-directed learning. The first, the more obvious of the two, is that self-directed learning means just what it says—the learner has substantial control over the purposes, the content, the form, and the pace of learning, and furthermore, the learner is the primary judge of when sufficient learning has occurred. Note that, easy as it is to declare the character of self-directed learning, this character points to a whole universe of attitudes and actions in the life of a learner—an alternative universe, indeed, to the one envisioned in institutional learning philosophy, with its strong belief in the learner's need for proper guidance if the learning process is not to waste time and other resources and the learner is not to acquire "bad habits."

Let me say it again: self-direction means substantial control over the purposes, content, form, and pace of learning and over evaluating when sufficient learning has occurred. With our tough-minded educator/manager hats on, we can all think of a thousand objections to this formulation, schooled as we are in institutional learning philosophy. Learning as a way of being asks us to think truly afresh about what we are really saying when we advocate self-directed learning.

The second and less obvious idea about self-directed learning is that it is a kind of conundrum. How can we know enough to direct our own learning process? Isn't self-directed learning just a polite phrase for blundering, floundering, and thrashing around in some unfamiliar territory of new material? Is this what learning as a way of being is advocating? The answer is no. Learning as a way of being admits the problem: there can certainly be periods in a self-directed learning process when we are blundering, when we are frustrated, losing motivation and getting demoralized, and beginning to look around for a quick fix or a magic bullet to dispel the confusion. At this critical moment, two things can occur: first, we can proceed to turn over substantial control of our learning's purpose, content, form, pace, and evaluation to someone else. This amounts to embracing institutional learning, to adopting a passive, dependent mentality that says, "Okay, teach me." Our experience with institutional learning has bred this response deeply into millions of us, and it is a reflex that we have to unlearn if we are going to take the second alternative and continue to practice learning as a way of being in a healthy way.

The second alternative also involves other people who know more, but when we are engaged in self-directed learning, our attitude toward these others (whether manifested as persons or as textbooks, software, or other material compiled by experts) is completely different. We seek help not from a position of dependency but on our own terms, and we are conscious of our self-directed stance. We have questions to ask the experts, questions that grow out of our experience to date with the material, frustrating as it has been. We have reasons, which remain conscious and clear, for wanting to continue to struggle with the learning. Our questions are *particular*; the expert may instruct us to "go back to chapter one," but the self-directed learner may not be ready to do that yet. The other-directed, dependent learner says, "Okay, I'm in your hands." The self-directed learner says, "Before we go back to the beginning, help me understand this diagram in chapter six." Logically, perhaps, we ought to begin at the beginning. Psychologically, however, we ought to begin where our energy and curiosity are. This is what learning as a way of being honors and institutional learning forgets.

Because it is so fundamental, self-directed learning will continually arise when we are engaged in the other six qualities of learning as a way of being. Indeed, we might hypothesize that self-directed learning is the natural state of human being; whereas other-directed learning (that is, learning caused and controlled by someone other than the learner) requires the learner to suppress any inner impulses to learn in another way. Other-directed learning, which institutional learning of course embodies, is thus a secondary state of human being—important for many kinds of learning to be sure but often not the first impulse within us. Ideally, other-directed learning would be a conscious self-initiated act, and much of it is. But much of it is not, including most of the learning presented to us in childhood through institutional learning mechanisms. It is no surprise, therefore, that self-directed learning feels inefficient to us and possibly the action of a renegade. We have been encouraged to think so from the dawn of our awareness of ourselves as learners.

One particular mode of self-directed learning that must be introduced here even though it is discussed at greater length in Chapter Four is self-directed learning for leadership. One of the supreme ironies of management education is that we have thought we could educate *leaders* through institutional learning, which keeps us in a passive, dependent state. Leadership training through institutional learning can be no more than talking *about* leadership as a subject while holding the learner firmly in institutional learning–sanctioned modes of conduct and performance criteria.

The relevance of self-directed learning to leadership is this: the behavior we call leadership is, before it is anything else, an initiative from within oneself. Leadership has self-direction as its essence, for to communicate to anyone else what ought to be done, a leader must first have communicated it, however loosely, to himself or herself. So the crucial learning process for a leader is learning what he or she wants to see happen. Leaders often seem to have—preformed—a brilliant answer or interpretation that they are urging on others. The learning process they went through to get to that position of clarity is hidden from their followers and, more importantly for our understanding of learning as a way of being, from subsequent learners who are trying to understand what it is leaders do. Leaders engage in complex and subtle learning processes about possible objectives, about resources for reaching them, and about barriers to be overcome—that is what they do *as leaders*. Learning leadership must therefore be learning about this complex and subtle learning process that a leader goes through over and over again. That process is a thoroughly self-directed affair, and thus learning for leadership must be self-directed learning.

Institutional learning philosophy and practice tend to miss this understanding of leadership. Institutional learning never gives us as learners a chance to feel a strong desire to make things go one way rather than another. It has rarely if ever figured out how to build that quality of strong desire into readings, lectures, and exercises about leadership. Yet without that abiding inner need to make something happen in an organization, the most critical element of leadership—its very essence—is left out of the learning process, and without that inner experience *and the opportunity to experiment with it,* all the theories and third-person cases about leadership that institutional learning teaches so well are beside the point.

Creative Learning (LWB1 + 2)

Creative learning is almost a contradiction in terms in the world of the institutional learning model. The essence of the institutional learning model is the idea that learning is the process of transferring information from one who knows to one who does not know. If there is no "body of knowledge" to be transferred, institutional learning does not know quite what to do. Permanent white water, however, presents problems that often require us to explore new areas of knowledge and skill that no one else has ever synthesized in quite this way before. As noted earlier, in permanent white water, we frequently feel we are "playing a whole new ball game," "writing the book as we go," "learning as we go." It takes courage to be comfortable with a learning process that we know is not following any established protocol, perhaps wandering down blind alleys or, worse yet, causing us to learn our way into error. Institutional learning has conditioned us all to feel nervous when we're not sure we are learning the "right thing."

Another word that captures creative learning is *exploration*. Exploratory learning cannot be sure exactly where it is going or how it will know when it has "gotten there," and that experience captures the reality of the learning situation in permanent white water perfectly. Exploratory learning is in conflict with one of the central canons of the institutional learning model—that in order for effective learning to occur there must be clear learning goals whose degree of attainment can be measured. If the model of institutional learning is right about that, then no effective learning can go on in permanent white water! In creative learning, exploration of the meaningfulness of the goal is *part of the learning itself*. Learning as a way of being is not against clear goals in general, but it is against arbitrary or meaningless clear goals. (For a further introduction to exploration, see Resource II, which pursues the idea of exploration through a fantasized conversation with one of the great explorers of the twentieth century).

The mistake we constantly make with creative products, especially as they are presented to us through institutional learning modes, is to assume that the creators had just these products in mind from the beginning. Then we feel awe that someone could have conceived of this creative entity in all its complexity and artfulness, and we conclude, wrongly, that we are witness to some kind of superhuman achievement. Indeed, it would be superhuman if a whole novel or symphony or building existed full-blown in the mind of its creator before any part of it was set down in some external form. But such is hardly ever the case. First, there is a learning process, which we do not see but by which the creator works out the implications and possibilities of the original starter concept (Ghiselin, 1952; Storr, 1972). This process is what the institutional learning model tends to obscure. Moreover, the word *creativity* has been so overworked that we forget what it is really saying, and we forget to look at the creative action from the point of view of the creator. The creative (learning) person may have a feeling or guiding image as work proceeds, but he or she does not know what is going to come out next or exactly what the final product is going to be. As one artist of my acquaintance has said, she knows that a project is finished "just before it starts to become something I have a name for." She is saying that as soon as she has a name for the work, further refinement will be replication of something she has recognized rather than continued creation. The refinement may be appropriate, but it is different in her mind from creativity.

When we are creating, we frequently surprise ourselves, and in that surprise *is* the learning. As they view the final result, creative people are often as astonished by what they have produced as are others. The downside to this truth about creativity is that it is a form of learning not really under our control. Of course, we can do a great deal of arranging of circumstances, hoping to enhance the chances for a creative breakthrough on a particular project. But all this arranging and enhancing can only increase probabilities; it cannot guarantee results. Furthermore, to compound the mystery, we know that our creative insights and actions often occur under the most improbable circumstances, when no one would have thought that a breakthrough was just around the corner. No, despite all the advice given about how to be more creative, the act of learning something no one else (as far as we know) has ever quite learned before under our specific circumstances is not programmable behavior.

Discomfort sometimes accompanies creative learning, but it is a different kind of pain from that imposed in institutional learning. Over time, institutional learning experiences convince us it is the *subject* that is the cause of our pain. We develop fears like "math anxiety" and "aversions" to one topic or another. However, the pain, boredom, fear, and anger we have all felt within institutional learning frameworks may more likely result from the system's oppressiveness than from the subject matter per se.

The pain of genuine creativity is self-directed, self-chosen pain. For example, the novelist Joyce Carol Oates, in explaining her own creative process, has said "[t]he practicing writer, the writer-at-work, the writer immersed in his or her project, is not an entity at all, let alone a person, but a curious mélange of wildly varying states of mind, clustered toward what might be called the darker end of the spectrum: indecision, frustration, pain, dismay, despair, remorse, impatience, outright failure" (Oates, 1983, p. 106). Just so. There is pleasure in the chase and delight in the outcome, but there is pain also. "Why do I do this to myself?" is the abiding question of the creative person—but we must not fail to notice the personal awareness: "I" do it.

If we think about experiences we have had as managers and leaders, we realize that the creativity required of us is quite different from what we usually mean by creativity, and the distinction is important for learning as a way of being. Usually, the word *creativity* describes the process of the individual as he or she comes up with new ideas and actions. It has a powerful connotation of individual action. However, much managerial literature insists that the manager is not a hands-on doer. Instead, he or she takes actions that direct and support the work of hands-on doers. What then is the creativity of the managerial leader? Managerial leaders are not so much concerned with creating things themselves as they are with creating *processes* among themselves and others that will result in new ideas occurring and new work being done. The creativity of the managerial leader is to shape ways of working, ways of structuring human relationships, ways of focusing and budgeting resources, ways of evaluating progress that do not kill it in the process.

What is the *learning* that goes with this work? Ironically, in recent years we have witnessed a retreat from even asking this question, let alone *creating* possible answers to it. Instead, we have seen an enormous increase in how-to-do-it books for managers. It is as if creativity has been factored out of the managerial equation, and that instead, managers are just supposed to copy someone else's list of do's and don'ts for the task of discovering what is possible among a group of people in an organization. To copy someone else's protocol is to make a decision not to be creative, and it is important to see this current obsession with how-to-do-it texts as a flight from creativity. It is a perfect example of how institutional learning has disempowered us for learning in permanent white water. There is no question that creative learning about the potentialities of new human relationships within the white water context is some of the most difficult learning a managerial leader can engage in. Nevertheless, it is learning that must be undertaken if organizations are going to navigate white water successfully.

Expressive Learning (LWB1 + 2 + 3)

"Learn by doing" is an old and hackneyed phrase, yet it embodies a profound truth: some things are best learned when we actually try to do them. Institutional learning philosophy grants that doing is important, but the practice of institutional learning often changes "learn by doing" into "do after learning." Expressive learning, however, is about doing things and learning in the process. Reading books about doing things, hearing about them from others, or watching others do them—while just imagining oneself acting—these experiences do not provide expressive learning. The institutional learning model has subtly altered the role of expressiveness from a learning mode to a way of "demonstrating" or "applying" something that has been learned in some other mode—presumably one of institutional learning's more structured and controlled settings.

Institutional learning does encourage expressive learning in a very few fields through what it calls experimentation. The learner is given hands-on exposure to the materials to be learned and is taught to manipulate those materials to produce hypothesized effects. Classroom experimentation, however, is a misleading surrogate for real experimentation. In real experimentation, we do not know what is going to happen; that is why we conduct the experiment. When we know what is going to happen, the event is better called demonstration. It would add to our understanding of the psychology of learning if we discovered just how much (or how little) the conducting of demonstrations under supervised conditions actually teaches a person about real experimentation. An experiment begins with the asking of an original question—a nice example of self-directed learning combined with creative learning—and continues with the experiment itself, which is expressive learning. The ability to ask original questions and imagine how they could be tested in action will not be developed by repeating someone else's experiment.

Expressive learning is crucial to one of the most interesting problems in learning—a problem that is especially important in learning managerial leadership: how do we learn the "big picture" or "gestalt" of any activity? From hang gliding to growing African violets to writing sonnets, the elements of an activity are not the activity itself. The only way to get a sense of the activity itself is to do it, however clumsily and haltingly. If we think about anything we personally are quite good at, we will probably discover that we engaged in this expressive, or "performing," quality of learning from very early in our involvement. It was not the elements that grabbed us; it was the whole activity. Of course, we realized that if we were going to realize our self-directed dream—say, to run the Boston Marathon—there were a whole lot of specific details we needed to understand and become competent in. But the dream was not in the details, it was in the larger picture. The learning of the meaning of the whole was what made the learning of the parts meaningful.

In expressive learning, we are not passively instructed in the subject. Instead, we learn the *roles* and the *timing* of the various elements in relation to each other (we know how all the parts go together, and we know why), we learn the *relationship* of the activity to the wider setting in which it occurs, and we learn how the activity is spread out in *time* as well as in space. That is, since most activities of any complexity occur in a time stream, we learn the pacing they require, their rhythms and durations. These are learnings we cannot attain merely by talking about an activity. At a deeper level than verbal description, we learn the *meaning* the activity has to its top performers, and we begin to incorporate those meanings as our own. We learn the *culture* of the activity. These learnings accumulate through *repeated* experiences with expressive learning; just a "taste" of the performing aspects won't do. This kind of learning is what Polanyi (1964) called "personal knowledge" and what William James called "knowledge-of-acquaintance" as contrasted with the impersonal "knowledge-about" something (Kaplan, 1961, p. 133). Heinlein found it necessary in his fiction to invent a new word entirely ("grokking") to capture a more profound kind of knowing and perceiving than is possible through ordinary consciousness (1961, p. 9). When we talk about "bone-deep" understandings and commitments of members in excellent organizations, we are talking about the same thing. We are describing learning that resonates in the total person in an integrated flow of mind, body, and spirit, no matter how humble or mundane the activity. It is the essence of learning as a way of being. (To jump ahead a bit, these modes of knowing are also part of feeling learning. In expressive learning, we are expressing our *feeling* for a situation, and learning is occurring at the level of our feelings as well as at our "head-level.")

Institutional learning philosophy and practice have always had difficulty with expressive learning. They grant that the learner needs an opportunity to experience ideas in action. They try to give the learner "exercises" that will seat these ideas deep in the learner's psyche and skill repertoire. But institutional learning is conflicted about learning that occurs expressively because its fundamental assumption is that cognitive content is the primary component of all learning. *Cognitive content* means ideas, concepts, theories, research findings, models—what institutional learning calls "the material." In the perpetual tug-of-war between time spent on "content" and time spent on "application," institutional learning consistently tends to opt for content, believing that there will be time later for practice. What institutional learning overlooks is that in so choosing, it lowers the learner's interest and capacity for later application. Thus, an enormous amount of content imparted through institutional learning modes decays and ultimately dies in the learner because the opportunity for expressive learning was sacrificed.

The situation I am describing is dramatically illustrated by the history of the field of experiential learning, as pioneered in the late 1950s by organizational behavior professors in U.S. business schools and developed continually since by a variety of educators both in higher education and in industry (see, for example, Back, 1972; Bennis and Schein, 1965; Bradford and others, 1964; Kolb, 1984). Experiential learning took a dramatic step beyond the prevailing institutional learning modes of one-way lecture supplemented by instructor-controlled "discussion." It put the learner in various problem-solving situations, usually with other learners and usually with the nominal instructor in a facilitator rather than a controller role, on the assumption that learning would occur through these experiences. However, even experiential learning has remained relatively anchored in institutional learning contexts, being seen as a "change of pace" or an "enrichment" of the subject being taught rather than as a separate learning vehicle that can impart learning experiences of different kinds and in different ways than can be done didactically. Furthermore, experiential learning has more and more become a vehicle to make a particular point to the learner rather than to provide the learner with a self-directed opportunity to explore (creative learning) ideas and relationships in action. Institutional learning has undercut the original spirit of experiential learning and converted it into a harmless adjunct to the main business of imparting content in an efficient and impersonal way.

Leading and managing were the original foci of experiential learning, and the regressive process just described can be clearly seen in the way these subjects have been learned. Leading and managing, especially in permanent white water, are extraordinarily complex flowing mosaics of attitude and action. Institutional learning has broken these processes into "elements" and fashioned various "experiential exercises" intended to impart the feel of some of the elements through expressive learning. The assumption has been that the elements will be added up later by the learner into an integrated performance. What institutional learning has forgotten is that the experts who break the act of leading and managing down into bite-sized elements already understand the gestalt of the integrated performance. Too often, though, the expert has not paid close enough attention to how he or she acquired that gestalt, with the result that the expert may not be able to evaluate whether or not the elements will add up to the gestalt for a learner who does not have the gestalt before the fact. Without the big picture, the learner does not know exactly what to pay attention to, and of course, the expert is blind to this blindness in the learner (Vaill, 1989a, chap. 7). Without the gestalt, expressive learning degenerates into "fun and games," as students have learned contemptuously to refer to experiential exercises. (The problem of how the crucial gestalt is acquired is solved when on-line learning, continual learning, and reflexive learning are interwoven, and this will be discussed further in Chapter Four.)

Even more unfortunate is the situation in which the expert does not possess the gestalt in the first place, having learned the elements as discrete factors and never having engaged in the expressive learning of using the elements in action. This is the familiar case of the management professor who has never managed anything, the academic doctor who does not see patients, the political analyst who has never run for office, the leadership theorist who has never exercised any leadership. Such educators tend to communicate only the fragmented parts of the overall leading and managing process. The whole never jells for the learner until long after the exposure to the content. Sometimes it never does.

Many who have taught management and leadership to beginners have noted that beginners often do *not* get the gestalt just from studying the abstracted elements. There is a leap the learner has to make from the parts to the whole. The learner takes this leap when he or she directly does the thing that has been taught. Especially in the dynamic, changing conditions of permanent white water, we cannot assume that a person can learn to function comfortably and effectively there—that is, take the leap—by reading about it, thinking about it, watching others doing it, performing somewhat far-fetched exercises around it, or just hoping that he or she will be able to muddle through when the time comes. After all, when we refer somewhat condescendingly to the "real world," isn't this the point we are making? Why not, instead, simply call the proverbial spade a spade and declare that learning for managerial leadership in permanent white water needs to be primarily expressive learning from the outset? Even if the learner is not fully engaged in learning in the real world, there is much more he or she can do on the expressive dimension than institutional learning typically allocates time for.

A pioneer in this point of view is Revans, with his process of *action learning* (Revans, 1986). In the United States, action learning means taking action in an organization, learning from the results, and incorporating that learning into further action. (This process is also often called *action research*.) Revans's idea of action learning is quite different: it is to create learning teams of working managers to work on real organizational problems and to structure the experience in such a way that both useful solutions to these problems emerge and substantial learning occurs for participants, learning that goes beyond the technical details of the particular problem. Interpersonal relationship learning occurs through group meetings as participants learn from each other and from those they must consult, historical learning occurs from seeing the problem through time, strategic learning occurs through seeing the problem in relation to broader organizational objectives and processes, and paradigmatic learning occurs through challenging underlying assumptions. In the process, traditional ways of doing things move from being sacred to being problematic; and in general, the whole matrix of policies and practices and ideas within which the problem resides become the objectives of group interaction and mutual learning. As Revans neatly sums up the concepts, "*real* people learn with and from other *real* people by working together in *real* time on *real* problems" (p. 75).

The theory and practice of action learning as Revans has developed it is an impressive achievement, and we can only hope that the recent surge of interest in it will continue (Dixon, 1994). What is striking though is that there are so few—if any—other examples in management and leadership education of learning systems that insist on the importance of expressiveness. The young men and women of today who will be the managerial leaders in the permanent white water of tomorrow receive practically no exposure to expressive learning in their formal education and training.

What does expressive learning look like? Ironically, we already know, except that we don't think of it as learning and we don't regard it as respectable enough for inclusion in institutional learning curricula about managerial leadership. Consider the following colloquial expressions that we might use to describe ourselves in certain circumstances:

- "Going with the flow"

- "Playing it by ear"

- "Taking things as they come"

- "Rolling with the punches"

- "Playing the hand I'm dealt"

- "Keeping my options open"

- "Hanging in there"

- "Making do with what I have"

- "Making lemonade out of lemons"

- "Reminding myself easy does it"

- "Crossing that bridge when I come to it"

- "Throwing away the script"

- "Feeling my way along"

- "Learning as I go"

- "Flying by the seat of my pants"

- "Keeping scrambling"

- "Playing it as it lays"

- "Taking things one day at a time"

There is a revolutionary metaphysics of learning in all these common phrases. When we use them to describe ourselves, they are code for "I'm in the midst of a learning process," while at the same time they convey our sense of the difficulties and complexities of a situation. What they show is that our experience of learning and coping with problems in the real time of organizational life is quite different from the abstract structured way that institutional learning talks about these same problems and how to solve them. All of us know what these colloquial metaphors mean in terms of learning. But they are not operational enough for institutional learning, which wants explicit objective statements about "managerial competencies" so that it has something to teach.

However, managers and other kinds of leaders have been fashioning descriptions of their competencies for generations, and the preceding list is a pretty good summary. These phrases capture the *feel* (the feeling learning) of expressiveness, the *experience* of trying to exert influence in complex evolving situations that defy all neat step-by-step protocols for taking action.

What is dramatic about all these phrases is that they contain a presumption that two things are going to happen to a managerial leader in the process of taking action. One is that the external world is not going to hold still; it is going to produce all kinds of surprises. (These surprises are simply the learnings of others about how to respond to the initiatives of the managerial leader!) The second thing that will happen is less prominent but equally important: the person taking the action is going to *learn* in the course of the experience and, after that, is going to see possibilities and constraints downstream that he or she could not see before. Some of the metaphorical phrases are clearer than others about this second kind of experience, but I think it is fair to say that all of them can be interpreted as containing this awareness that action in complex systems has to balance, reconcile, and integrate change on the outside with change (learning) on the inside.

Organizational learning is not a phenomenon of recent invention. Human organizations have always been the sites of nonstop learning by everyone in them. Ironically, therefore, though expressive learning is consistently given short shrift by institutional learning, it is at the core of all organizational learning and, as such, is of central importance to any managerial leader.

Feeling Learning (LWB1 + 2 + 3 + 4)

The qualities of learning as a way of being already discussed—self-directed learning, creative learning, and expressive learning—clearly involve learning that is much more than merely cognitive intellectual attainment. Probably none of those three qualities are possible for us if we are not able to feel learning happening within ourselves and honor it, respond to it, build on it. Self-directed learning, creative learning, and expressive learning all involve a whole range of feelings, among which curiosity, patience, courage, and self-esteem are particularly important. Inevitably, negative feelings arise also (as Joyce Carol Oates, quoted previously, made excruciatingly clear).

The basic point about feeling learning in learning as a way of being is that we need to develop self-acceptance of the feelings that arise during learning because these feelings are part of the learning. They are not, as institutional learning would have it, annoyances that must be put up with in the learning process. Rather, the feeling of learning is one of the most reliable signals we could want that learning is occurring!

An unfortunate dichotomy has been seen in recent years between so-called cognitive learning and affective learning, as if we or someone leading us could control where in our personality and brain our learning is absorbed, stored, and subsequently utilized. Put this way, the dichotomy is obviously absurd. I believe that it was perceived, though, in reaction to the emphasis on cognitive learning in the institutional learning model, learning supposed to qualify as "true knowledge." Because institutional learning ignores or actively suppresses the feeling side of learning, a countermovement has arisen over perhaps the last thirty years that aims to give learners an opportunity to experience learning different from cognitive knowledge. Thus, we have "nonverbal learning," "body work," "poetic learning," the "language of the senses," "deep knowing," and so forth. I am not questioning the validity of any of these developments. Rather, I am questioning the dichotomy and suggesting that we should employ modes of learning that are not premised on it. The watchword should be that all learning has both cognitive and affective aspects and that both should be equally honored. We should not have to suppress one or the other to be consistent with some doctrine of main learning objectives.

Furthermore, in permanent white water, learning is not restricted to facts and methods. We are also possessed of learning attitudes— attitudes of curiosity, courage, trust, self-respect, tough-mindedness, optimism, and an ability to keep a sense of perspective. This is a point forgotten in institutional learning, and that is regrettable; in learning for white water, feelings are learned every bit as much as are ideas and skills. Perhaps in a stable, predictable environment, we can focus on absorbing information and practicing skills without worrying much about attitudes—figuring that we can develop these later. But in a turbulent environment, we cannot know what our learning *means* if we do not develop positive attitudes and feelings about it at the same time. When I say that institutional learning does not prepare young people for the world of work, this is what I mean: they may have the facts and methods, but they do not have the attitudes and feelings they need to function effectively; and without these attitudes and feelings, the facts and methods are useless.

Feeling learning is one of the most important modes of learning as a way of being because the pace, pressure, and complexity of permanent white water can leave us distracted, anxious, and breathless. Millions of us go through years of intensive learning in the institutional learning mode without ever getting much help in feeling and internalizing what we are learning and what we know. The institutional learning model tends to omit all the deeper modes of learning and knowing and the help we need with these, not because the philosophy of institutional learning denies the existence of the deeper modes so much as that it lacks methods for conducting learning at this level. Learning as a way of being is learning by a whole person, and that means feeling the learning as well as possessing it intellectually.

Feeling learning probably is one of the most important factors in retention of what is learned. Maybe the reason information we "cram" is retained only for a short period is that we do not develop our feeling for the material but try only to remember it on a technical level. Feeling learning also enormously enriches the learning experience. Even institutional learning expresses this in one of its favorite clichés, the "love of learning." Love of learning is *real*, and it is essential. But institutional learning does not know how to develop it.

On-Line Learning (LWB1 + 2 + 3 + 4 + 5)

Mainstreaming is the term invented for the process of deinstitution-alizing individuals whose problems have been perpetuated and even exacerbated rather than alleviated because the individuals have been permanently housed within all-encompassing institutions. Learning in the institutional learning mode is not mental illness, but it is learning profoundly stunted by all the institutional restric-tions we encounter from kindergarten right through the Ph.D. and beyond in continuing education environments. Thanks to the com-puter revolution, the term *on-line* has come into currency to de-scribe a process that occurs simultaneously with all the other processes of the system in which it is imbedded. Thus, on-line learn-ing is a learning process that occurs in the midst of work and of life rather than in an artificial, sheltered environment.

Some learning needs to take place in an organized educational setting controlled by someone other than the learner. But in our world of permanent white water, we need to find ways for as much learning as possible to occur on the job and in all other aspects of a learner's life. Listen to Gardner's memorable formulation of this idea: "The ultimate goal of the educational system is to shift to the individual the burden of pursuing his own education. This will not be a widely shared pursuit until we get over our odd conviction that education is what goes on in school buildings and nowhere else. Not only does education continue when schooling ends, but it is not confined to what may be studied in adult education courses. The world is an incomparable classroom, and life is a memorable teacher for those who aren't afraid of her" (1964, p. 12). Not only is this a ringing endorsement of on-line learning, it honors all the other qualities of learning as a way of being as well.

It is virtually a commonplace that on-the-job training is an extremely effective way to learn anything. Given that, it is some-what of a mystery—an odd conviction, as Gardner says—why we are not pushing as much learning into the mainstream as we can—

a mystery, at least, until the power of institutional learning ideology is recalled.

On-line learning is at the core of action learning as developed over the years by Revans (1986) (discussed previously under expressive learning). What is surprising, though, and what gives significance to on-line learning as a way of being, is that there are so few *other* philosophies and methods that seek to do what Revans's does. Why isn't on-line learning one of the most thoroughly developed ideas in education? Why aren't there multiple schools of thought about how to get the learning process out into the worlds of the learner's work, family, and recreation? Why isn't Gardner's observation an absolute *commonplace* instead of a piece of rare wisdom constantly obscured by the pretensions of institutional learning philosophy?

If we are serious about learning as a way of being, then we have to get learning out of artificial learning environments. It is ironic that this conclusion comes right at a time when literally billions of dollars are being spent by school systems, by corporations, and by all kinds of other organizations to design what they consider optimal learning environments, in which all kinds of advanced technologies are being installed. Innovative classrooms are being drawn up. That ancient vehicle of learning, the textbook, is undergoing a revolution as it incorporates computer software, video supplements, on-line linkages to authors, and other accoutrements. Granted, much of this work attempts to simulate powerfully the mainstream world. But since it is occurring within a framework of control and instruction (that is, structuring in), we can expect that over time all these innovations will acquire the formalisms and the rigidities of other institutional learning devices and we, as learners, will be right back where we were before, passively waiting to have learning experiences provided to us. The spirit of Gardner's insight will have been defeated again.

Taking care not to equate learning as a way of being with carefully defined learning environments is important for another reason as well. Permanent white water is inundating our once-tranquil off-line environments even as it is inundating the work place. The ivory tower is no longer a serene place for reflection. Support systems, such as libraries, are fraught with their own disruptions. Muggers may prowl quiet parks and other out-of-the-way places. Phones ring and fax machines whir. Jet noise reverberates. Most of us have had the experience of trying to carve out a quiet space for ourselves on a Sunday afternoon only to be disturbed constantly by noise, interruptions from others, and the press of our own time-dominated lives. Conducting an effective off-line learning process is itself an exercise in navigating white water; not that it cannot be done, but its certainty cannot be guaranteed.

But perhaps the collapse of once-tranquil off-line learning environments has a hidden benefit. Maybe learning to learn in the cacophony of the modern high school or college is practical preparation for learning as a way of being in the modern work organization! Perhaps under our noses the last few years, some modes of learning have been going on that our traditional assumptions have not equipped us to see. Institutional learning criteria for effective learning would say that the contemporary college dorm with its noise and its drugs and its sexual preoccupations and its cross-cultural swirl is no place to study. But perhaps that assumption needs to be reconsidered. In the world of work, we have similarly assumed that learners need to get off site, into the sort of protected environment described at the beginning of Chapter One. Can the modern organization itself be a stimulating and effective, rather than distracting and frustrating, learning environment? And if so, how?

If this notion has validity, then once again we can ask whether it might help if we recognized this fact about learning environments. Real learning does not require acres of grass, a carillon tolling softly in the distance, intimate small classes, and tweedy personable mentors. It is involuntary reluctant learning that needs these encouragements. Learning that comes out of true curiosity and commitment can proceed in airport boarding areas, the back seats of taxicabs, and customer service lines. Only a very few scholarly pursuits require huge library collections of arcane material; most learning can be conducted out of the materials available at any good bookstore or newsstand. Or to put it a little differently, to the extent that our traditional assumptions about learning environments do not define the contents of a good trade bookstore or fully stocked newsstand as intellectually challenging, our sensitivity to the amount of learning that can go on in such environments is dulled. Of course, we frequent these settings—spend hours in them, many of us—but do we consciously think of this activity as a crucial part of our learning process and intellectual development? Do we officially measure the quality of a university by the number of bookstores that surround it or by the library it maintains? Does one go to Harvard for access to Harvard Square? We do not have good ways of talking about the mainstream learning environments that surround universities, even though we all know what extraordinary varieties and amounts of learning occur there.

So much learning is not programmed by anyone in particular, not focused on objectives someone else supplied, not carefully structured and modularized in sequential "units." This is the on-line, feeling, expressive, creative, self-directed learning that we perform on and within ourselves for ourselves because the world of white water has made it necessary for us to learn constantly, effectively, and enjoyably, to take part in learning as a way of being.

Continual Learning (LWB1 + 2 + 3 + 4 + 5 + 6)

Learning as a way of being has to be a lifelong continual process. In this respect, it is in accord with our traditional assumptions about learning. *Lifelong learning* is such an appealing phrase that it has become virtually a cliché in contemporary America. Many familiar aphorisms—"You never stop learning"; "You're never too old to learn"; "You learn something new everyday"—reinforce the notion.

But have we thought carefully enough about what continual learning really means? For one thing, it means continually exploring the meaning of all the qualities of learning as a way of being, not just for their singular meanings but for how they interrelate—triggering and energizing each other, creating tensions, contradictions, and paradoxes for each other. In other words, it means continually exploring learning as a way of being as a *system*. Continual learning is nothing less than a developmental process of learning as a way of being. It is certainly never over or complete; a learner can never be sure that he or she has made hardly more than a start. The more fully a person achieves learning as a way of being, the more he or she will see that there is more to learn and will also see that the learning can be undertaken in the comfort of a fuller and fuller realization of this way of being.

Continual learning entails the difficult psychological achievement of open-mindedness. In an exact if rather dry definition, Rokeach has captured the essence of open-mindedness: it is the "extent to which a person can receive, evaluate, and act on relevant information received from outside on its own intrinsic merits unencumbered by irrelevant factors in the situation arising from within the person or from the outside" (1960, p. 57). What happens to so many of us, of course, is that we lose freshness and openness of perception as our learning accumulates and accretes, as we come to see ourselves as knowing a lot. The institutional learning model has taught us to think of learning this way, in building-block terms. We have been receiving powerful messages from the dawn of our awareness that we must get out of the beginner mode and into the mode of competent performer as quickly as possible. We are all deeply programmed to believe that learning is a process of "getting it right" (or perhaps I should say, "getting it righter and righter"), whether we are talking about toilet training, finger painting, or strategic management. Many people, in fact, would probably be astonished at the suggestion that learning can have any other purpose than to get better and better, "righter and righter."

However, permanent white water keeps posing surprises and novelties to us, things we have never faced before and often things no one has faced before. As noted in the previous chapter, white water thus makes perpetual beginners of us all. Almost nothing we have learned is immune from challenge and change, which means we had better be prepared to undergo the sometimes painful process of admitting that much of our past learning is obsolete, and returning to the beginner mode.

It is well for us to pause and think carefully about this idea of being continually catapulted back into the beginner mode, for that is the real meaning of being a continual learner. There seems to be no doubt that it happens. As I pointed out earlier, everywhere we go in the worlds of managerial leaders, we hear the same thing: "It's a whole new ball game." "We're reinventing ourselves." "It's back to square one for us." "We're writing the book as we go." "It's business as *unusual*." In fact, these off-hand references have become so common that we may not hear them for what they are: descriptions of the condition of being a beginner, and since we are in a world of *permanent* white water, we are going to be beginners indefinitely. Indeed, it is not an exaggeration to suggest that everyone's state of "beginnerhood" is only going to deepen and intensify *so that ten years from now each of us will be even more profoundly and thoroughly settled in the state of being a perpetual beginner.* With tongue only slightly in cheek, then, we may say that we are all at the peak of our powers today, that the rest of our careers will be a progressive process of our feeling more and more like beginners, of not being too sure exactly what we are doing, or why, or with what significance. We do not need competency skills for this life. We need *in*competency skills, the skills of being effective beginners.

Is it meaningful to speak of "learning to be a beginner"? The popular connotation of the word beginner almost precludes that idea. Yet if we buy the notion that our macrosystems do keep confronting us with novel ideas and problems, if we buy that a succession of ideas and problems will go on indefinitely, and finally, if we buy that these ideas and problems will have high stakes and time constraints, then we must also buy that the beginner role will be ours for the indefinite future and that we had better learn to function in it as effectively and comfortably as we can. Lifelong learning is therefore not merely life-long learning of such subject matter as "computers," or "culture," or "legislation"; it is lifelong learning about learning as well. Feeling learning as a way of being deals with what the content of such learn-ing might be. The discussion below of reflexive learning as a way of being will help us think further about the process of lifelong learning.

Consider a reflective beginner—someone who thinks about what it is to be a beginner and over time improves his or her abil-ity to be a beginner. What might be some of the key "incompeten-cies" of such a person? Here are some hypotheses:

- A reflective beginner is conscious of the learning process itself and is able to engage in a continual process of learning about learning.

- A reflective beginner is able to ask for help without embarrassment or apology and is able to be nonresent-fully dependent on someone who has more knowledge or experience.

- A reflective beginner is able to separate his or her over-all feeling of self-worth from personal deficiencies on a particular learning project.

- A reflective beginner is able to see the learning process as continual experimentation rather than as a system that gives the learner only one or two chances to "get it right."

- A reflective beginner understands the peculiar commu-nication problems that arise when a person with a lot of expertise tries to communicate with a nonexpert— how the expert often forgets that the beginner does not have the overall understanding within which particular facts and techniques can be fitted. (I have named this phenomenon *Satchmo's paradox*, after Louis Armstrong's famous reply upon being asked what jazz is: "Man, if you gotta ask, you'll never know.")

- A reflective beginner can recognize other beginners (even though they may be trying to hide their status) and be supportive of them rather than regarding them with indifference and/or falling into competition with them.

- A reflective beginner is able to maintain a sense of humor about the sometimes lamentable state of beginnerhood.

- A reflective beginner knows that feeling of wanting a cookbook, five easy steps, a magic bullet, anything to cut through the confusion, and knows the temptations and the dangers of this feeling.

- A reflective beginner has internalized the profound truth of "one day at a time," that is, he or she is relatively patient while living with and through a learning process that at times seems to be going nowhere.

Rokeach's definition of open-mindedness clearly involves the willingness to be a beginner, to treat whatever is before you as a fresh experience "unencumbered," as Rokeach says, "by irrelevant factors in the situation arising from within the person or from the outside." In much the same way, Suzuki (1979) speaks of "Zen mind, beginner's mind" as the ability to experience the world free of the attachments, assumptions, and unconscious evaluations that often result from past learnings, learnings that our institutional learning programming has convinced us are reliable building blocks for the future. They are not so in permanent white water; maybe not so, period, if one accepts the Zen doctrine. And finally, Gustav Mahler, that tortured soul, tells us how in his own struggle to express the enormous visions and passions that filled him, he found that "any routine that one has developed is useless; one always has to start learning from scratch to achieve anything new. In this way one always remains a *beginner!*" (Domling, 1991).

Reflexive Learning (LWB1 + 2 + 3 + 4 + 5 + 6 + 7)

The institutional learning model, to retain its power, needs to remain tacit in the learner's mind. It makes a lot of assumptions about what is good for the learner that a learner might well object to or want to renegotiate if given the opportunity. The institutional learning model is built in part on an implicit belief that learners should not bother with philosophical considerations about that model. A great majority of us, therefore, have lived most of our lives without any encouragement to think about images of learning and the philosophies of learning we are practicing. Nor have we been encouraged to assume that we can, indeed should, consciously vary the conditions of our learning to fit our preferred modes, the particular subject matter involved, and the surrounding environment.

Just consider some of the ideas, patterns, and assumptions we might be more aware of if our formal instruction had given us more encouragement to learn about ourselves as learners—that is, to practice reflexive learning.

• We would have ideas about the modes in which we do and do not learn effectively, about ways of experimenting with learning methods, about similarities and differences between the way one person learns and the way others learn. We would be able to connect our initial motivation to learn something with our subsequent experience of learning it, and we would be able to connect that experience to different so-called learning outcomes—skills attained, concepts grasped, grades received, and the like.

• We might be better able now to consider the many ways in which learning challenges and opportunities are changing. We have to know something about learning in the first place to detect the learning opportunities that are arising out of the information revolution, multicultural learner groups, holistic or "right-brained" approaches to learning, and mass communication technologies.

- We might be better prepared to cope more effectively with the inevitable pains, frustrations, and disappointments that accompany any learning process; that is, we might already have learned quite a bit about becoming better and better beginners (as discussed in relation to continual learning as a way of being).

- We might have some insights into the limits of efficiency in any learning process; that is, we might know how justified we are in any learning project in expecting to learn exactly what we need to know in exactly the fashion that will make it most useful to us and durable in our memories.

- We might be in a better position to enjoy learning for its own sake.

- We might eventually be in a pretty good position to help others reflect on their learning, which would become important preparation for their managerial leadership in the white water world.

- Finally, we might, had we spent more time observing ourselves as learners, find that these and many other awarenesses had become part of our normal consciousness of ourselves; that is, learning as a way of being might already be a central part of our sense of who we are and of what is going on in us constantly.

Human consciousness is naturally reflexive: it notices itself, and it notices itself noticing itself. It thinks about itself. Reflexivity in learning as a way of being is a natural process, and the ideas and insights just suggested will occur naturally if the restrictive philosophy of the institutional learning model is removed. The "double-loop learning" that Argyris has written about so penetratingly over the past two decades (Argyris and Schön, 1978) is about reflexivity, as are the earlier discoveries of the phenomenologists, beginning with Husserl (Husserl, 1970; Lawson, 1985; Zaner, 1970).

Learning to reflect on our own learning, therefore, is an enormously important part of learning as a way of being. There is also another, more direct focus for reflexivity and that is the seven qualities of learning as a way of being. As I have been illustrating, these modes are not independent of each other; they overlap and interrelate in countless ways. They constitute a *system*, not a list of independent factors. Therefore, the process of learning about learning must include reflexive learning of the interrelationships, mutual dependencies, reciprocal enrichings, and indeed possibly the tensions and trade-offs among the seven qualities.

The Practice of Continual Learning: Looking Back and Looking Forward

Learning as a way of being contains wonderful opportunities for reflexive learning, that is, for learning about learning. And the failure of institutional learning to develop learning-about-learning abilities in us looms as an ever greater tragedy as we contemplate the years so many of us have been induced to waste, pounding away at learning projects we did not understand, did not enjoy, and did not know how to transform into something more enjoyable and productive of growth. But we still have many opportunities to develop these abilities and transform our current learning. And I should note that if you have gotten this far in this book, you are probably someone who has survived demeaning orchestrations of your learning, someone who retains a curiosity about the process, who enjoys continuing to grow in learning, and who loves "that ole learnin' feelin'." That's what learning as a way of being is! There are many of you; nevertheless, I think you are the exception. If you were the majority, institutional learning would not continue to operate.

We can begin our learning about learning simply by asking just what it is. What is there to reflect upon in our experiences as learners? How do we know when we are reflecting? How do we focus our thinking in such a way as to be reflexive? To say that learning is reflexive is to say that it generates learning about itself even as it accomplishes the act we call learning and even though we may not be paying attention to this learning about learning or may actually have our attention diverted from it by the practices of institutional learning.

The question of the nature of reflexivity has occupied philosophers and psychologists for centuries and produced no certain answers. However, for our purposes of developing learning as a way of being as a practical frame of mind, undertaking a philosophical analysis of reflexivity is less important than having the ability to do it productively in the real time of living. It is this real-time learning about learning that reflexive learning as a way of being is about. Moreover, once we understand the practical function of reflexive learning, we can see that learning about learning is precisely determining the extent to which any learning activity possesses the first six qualities—to what extent is it self-directed, creative, expressive, feeling, on-line, and continual? In other words, we practice reflexive learning by reflecting on the modes of learning as a way of being, asking ourselves how these modes are manifest in our learning and, presumably, seeking to increase the presence of these modes in our learning as time goes on.

More specifically, we can ask the following kinds of questions about each mode.

Self-directed learning. To reflect upon our self-directed learning, we can ask about the extent to which we are directing our own learning as opposed to being dependent on someone else or drifting from one learning experience to the next, perhaps rather unconsciously. We can think back over the attitudes within us and circumstances outside us that seem to encourage rather than discourage self-direction. We can resolve to increase the amount of self-direction in our learning and think through what it is going to take to achieve an increase. We can note that the more we do creative, expressive, and on-line learning, the more likely it is that we will engage in self-directed learning. Creativity, expressiveness, and involvement in work applications virtually require self-directedness. Most of all, we can spell out achievable learning goals for ourselves and think through the methods we will employ to reach those goals. In all these reflexive activities, we are trying to understand how to increase our personal sense of ownership in our learning.

Creative learning. As we reflect upon creative learning, we can ask how much of our learning is just absorbing and repeating the learning of others versus pushing into areas that, as far as we know, are relatively unexplored. Are we "writing the book" as much as we are reading someone else's book? Are we cultivating the *feeling* (the feeling learning) of creating our learning as we go? Or are we simply incorporating predigested chunks (institutional learning says "modules") of someone else's creative learning? One particularly interesting effect of creative learning is that when it is occurring we *know* it is. Unlike absorptive learning, where we cannot be sure whether we have really gotten the point our teacher intended, creative learning is *ours*.

Expressive learning. We can reflect upon our expressive learning fairly easily because we recognize it easily (or perhaps we know it by its absence easily). The opposite of expressive learning is passivity, "just sitting there," often in a classroom of some sort, not knowing whether we can do what the learning is about or not. Expressive learning is self-demonstrative. In reflecting on it, we may find that our chief problem is not taking it seriously enough. We have been trained to think learning *is* passive absorption. On reflection, we may find ourselves repeatedly passing up opportunities to learn expressively.

Feeling learning. Reflection on feeling learning as a way of being involves, as the saying goes, "getting in touch with our feelings." The goal of reflection on feeling learning is, at any given moment, to be aware of both the feelings that infuse our learning *and* the continuing problems we have with feeling learning, since our institutional learning has trained us not to take too seriously the feelings we have while learning. Various learning experiences may trigger various feelings in us; the task is to identify the types of experiences and feelings that are characteristic for us, a task that is a part of the reflexive learning process. Reflection will introduce us to both pleasant and unpleasant feelings. When we encounter the unpleasant ones, like boredom, anger, confusion, and fear, we may find ourselves denying the significance of these feelings for our learning. After all, we have been trained to go through with a learning project regardless of what we feel about it. What we learn from our reflexive learning will possibly conflict directly with that training.

On-line learning. Reflection on on-line learning is to help us become learners who more and more inquire into all sorts of subjects all the time, under all kinds of conditions, and in connection with all sorts of projects with all kinds of people. In a sense, on-line learning ought to be one of the easiest of the qualities to develop, since the world presents us with such an incredibly rich array of learning opportunities. One would have to work hard to find a mainstream environment in which extraordinary amounts of learning were *not* possible. But reflexive learning about on-line learning has its dilemmas, too. We want the other five qualities of learning as a way of being also to be operating in the mainstream in which we are engaged in on-line learning, so we should ask ourselves the extent to which our on-line learning in the mainstream is self-directed, creative, expressive, feeling, and/or continual. Because the modern mainstream is permanent white water, it is easy to let ourselves be borne along by the diversity and excitement and to practice a de facto learning strategy of osmosis. Therefore, reflexive learning is of great importance if we are to take as full advantage of on-line learning opportunities as we can.

Continual learning. Continual learning presents a variety of reflexive opportunities. We can look back on our learning experiences of recent months and ask ourselves just how continual they have been so far. Have we plateaued in our learning? Are there areas of learning—picking up a foreign language, for example—in which we have been procrastinating? Do we hit learning dry spells where, despite a plethora of learning opportunities, we just seem to want a respite from conscious deliberate learning for a while? Perhaps that is the sense in which a vacation is supposed to be a "vacating." We need to attend to the way continual learning can become distorted if its pace is too rapid, a constant possibility in today's macrosystems. Not even the institutional learning model exactly recommends cramming, but for a variety of reasons, we find ourselves in that mode constantly—trying to read too much in too little time, pass a test we are inadequately prepared for, pick up a complex skill in record time, learn the ropes of an organization in a one-day orientation, and so forth. Reflection on our continual learning will help us understand how time-dependent learning really is: what its rhythms and accents are; how it interweaves with other evolving processes in our lives; how it has its seasons.

Before closing this lengthy meditation on the nature of learning as a way of being, I wish to share two other expressions of reflexive learning that also illustrate what learning about learning can be like. Both pertain specifically to learning about managerial leadership. The first asks learners to look back on past experiences, and the other asks them to look forward to anticipated experiences.

One very effective way to see learning as a way of being operating as a whole composed of all its qualities is to start from the outcome end and look back. When we account for our own learning process with respect to something we have gotten quite good at, that process often turns out to be not only very illuminating but also quite different from what the institutional learning model says learning is supposed to look like. For a number of years, I have asked managers and other professionals in my classes and workshops to focus on anything they can honestly say they are pretty good at, literally anything, and answer two questions about it.

1. What has been the process of your learning, that is, what is the stream of ideas and experiences that your learning has been composed of that brings you to your present degree of understanding and ability?
2. Why have you engaged in this learning process (think of both your original motives and the motives that have kept you going along the way)?

My data are not as systematic as I would like, but I have discovered some recurrent themes in the way people talk about successful learning processes, and these themes offer insights into learning as a way of being and suggest hypotheses for further inquiry. (If you like, reflect for a few minutes on your own answers to these questions before proceeding.)

All seven dimensions of learning as a way of being arise in people's accounts of their own learning. This is an interesting finding in itself: when asked to talk about their own successful learning, people routinely mention these modes. And what emerges most clearly in their answers to the two questions is how very personal people experience their successful learning process to have been, even when an external observer finds nothing exceptional in the way they came to attain competence. They were not copying someone else, not following someone else's protocol (thus, their learning was self-directed). Some say they were not even conscious of other ways to learn their chosen subject or activity than the way they were using. In some cases, the learning process had the quality of being a secret about the learners—something they were doing that no one else knew about. These latter people talked as though their learning felt almost like a conspiracy. People's answers also had very much the flavor of their letting the learning happen to themselves, of their not consciously engineering the learning. By no means was there indifference about progress; in fact, in many cases, a person almost desperately wanted to become competent in a chosen area. This letting-it-happen feeling often came up when people were talking about all the accidental or unplanned experiences that had contributed to their learning: how they ran into someone on an airplane "and got to talking," how they came across a key piece of literature while they were looking for something else, how they enrolled in some workshop at the last minute or attended a certain function just on a whim. One learner with a lifelong interest in sailing dated his first intense experience of that interest to repairing a model sailboat he had found in a pile of trash in the attic of a house his family had moved into when he was nine. As I have looked over people's learning experiences, my sense is very much that they had a succession of relatively unplanned experiences that were enormously fruitful. It is my impression that what goes unsaid is their feeling of continual discovery (the result of feeling learning and continual learning) and their pleasure and indeed delight in it. (As noted at the end of Chapter One, it is people experiencing a successful learning project whom teachers love to work with—if, that is, there happens to be a conjunction between what the teacher is teaching and what the learner is personally excited about—precisely because these people have a delight in learning.)

Among the people who answered my two questions, the original motivation for getting involved in a learning project was extremely variable. "Accident" is probably the most common explanation—accident of where one lived, of something a friend (or an attractive member of the opposite sex) was doing, of a hand-me-down book or set of tools or athletic equipment, of a chance meeting with a celebrity. The motivation that these people report is that the activity is self-justifying (the psychologist's term is *autotelic*). We do learn things for future purposes, but when people are asked to describe why they got involved in some subject or activity where they have attained mastery as they define it, learning for future payoff is not often mentioned. They will say they never thought of *not* doing it; they talk of taking to it like a duck to water, of not being able to imagine what their lives would be like without this thing in it.

Remember that this is not a general discussion of what motivates learning but rather an exploration of how people describe learning experiences they feel have been highly successful. Remember, too, that the institutional learning model does not presume all this intrinsic motivation that people report. Institutional learning is prone to motivation by the carrot and the stick, which is not at all surprising, by the way. Institutional learning relies on so many conditions and norms that are unnatural for learners that an external framework of rewards and punishments is virtually mandatory to keep learners on track. The people whose learning I am describing, though, do not describe their ongoing motivation as inspired by others' carrots and sticks; they keep themselves on track.

One very interesting characteristic of the learning processes these people report is the role that books and concepts and formal techniques played. By no means did most of these successful learners shy away from information on their subjects that was available in libraries, courses, or other formal experiences. In fact, many were inventive in finding ways to acquire formal training on a low budget and/or a tight schedule (exhibiting creative, on-line, and continual learning). What is striking is their mood as they approached these more formal sources. It was what we call today an empowered mood; they had a full sense of *why* they were taking the course or reading the book, because it had been their own decision to do so (another example of self-directed learning). They had, again in a current term, ownership of the learning process. They were not waiting for someone to tell them why they should be interested in the subject. They didn't have to be sold on the value of the subject or its intrinsic interest. They had already experienced enough of it in their own way to know it was for them.[2]

Doubtless plenty of learners are presold on various subjects by parents, friends, and teachers and yet go on to attain high competence. In professions requiring long training, such as medicine, there are probably many highly competent practitioners who had the field sold to them first and then set out to learn it. Nevertheless, the sequence in which self-discovery of the intrinsic interest and importance of a subject or skill *precedes* formal learning experiences is not the sequence in which institutional learning philosophy presumes learning should occur. In institutional learning, the learner is given the objectives and then is instructed to follow a carefully planned

2. It is a commonplace in adult education that adults tend to know their reasons for taking a course or otherwise studying a subject. But the institutional learning model still permits an instructor to stand up in front of adult learners and act as though they have no idea why they are in that room studying that subject. In advising the instructor to state the objectives of the course, the model actually encourages the instructor to ignore the learners' own reasons for being there.

program (once again, the program is in-structed, that is, structured in). According to the philosophy, this is how learners come to love their subject and how they attain high competence. Yes, some do; millions do not.

Another characteristic of the self-described successful learners I have questioned is their diffidence. It is as if they know that by the world's standards they are very good at whatever they are discussing, and they accept this, but they do not feel particularly competent. In fact, many communicate distinct feelings of incompetence, ineptness, clumsiness, of being "hardly more than a beginner." And this may be a world-class athlete or a Nobel prize winner talking. Their love for their subject and their immersion in its intricacies is humbling and awe inspiring. These people take no smug pleasure in getting A's in their subject or having honors heaped on them. The general public hardly takes it seriously when a Jack Nicklaus, a Jessye Norman, or a Michael Jordan says he or she is still just trying to get the fundamentals right. But I am convinced, after listening to a lot of successful learners talk about their learning processes, that such demurrals are genuine and not just for show, not just false humbleness. The film director and screenwriter Nora Ephron recently said of her craft, "The more you do it, the harder it gets, because you just learn how bad you are!" (Ephron, 1994). Artists who really know what they know are also awed by what they do not know, even when what they do not know is invisible to the layperson. This mix of feelings about competence integrates feeling, continual, and reflexive learning in a striking way.

Awe and humbleness are also real in a learner who is centered in the process (practicing feeling, on-line, and continual learning), for what is yet to be learned is experienced as unlimited. The learning can go on for as long as one is willing to engage in it (continual learning), no matter how mundane and ordinary the content in the eyes of the world. Inspired learners know what many of the great religions have long preached: depth of personal meaning and significance of work is not a function of its worldly importance. Real lifelong learning (feeling learning and continual learning) is not a slogan on a conference brochure but a felt future adventure that needs no further justification.

Most of the learners I work with are aspiring to be managerial leaders. I have asked them a third question in addition to the two about their learning processes and reasons for engaging in them.

> 3. Now that you have identified some key things about how and why you attained high competency in this thing you've been focusing on, consider—to what extent are these principles and experiences occurring in the way that you are learning management and leadership?

The answers to this question are not nearly so positive. People report that they cannot connect what they are studying to what they think managing and leading people in organizations is like, that is, they are being denied both feeling and on-line learning. In their own way, they are confirming all the critiques of management education that have appeared recently pointing to how technique-oriented the curricula and the training programs are, how detached from the human beings supposedly being led and managed, how awash in quantitative analysis and computer applications. In addition, material is by and large presented in a straight lecture-discussion mode with a textbook as the main resource, that is, expressive learning is being denied these learners. "This doesn't feel like what I think management and leadership must be," say these future managers, even though they tend not to be able to say in much detail what they would like to see changed. But this inability is yet another characteristic of the system that supports institutional learning—the conferring on the subject matter expert of an almost godlike status and the companion hesitancy by the learner to suggest that this god-expert does not know how to present the subject matter effectively. Even the learner who positively knows that the subject is incompetently presented, despite the instructor's technical qualifications, usually hesitates to suggest alternative modes out of reluctance to risk a fight with the presenter. We know when we are not learning, even if we are not sure what changes would facilitate our learning. So we keep quiet.

It has proved very fruitful to ask about the learning process of learners who feel good about their learning on some subject. Institutional learning, it turns out, is a deficiency-oriented model, almost in the same sense as Herzberg's famous "satisfier" factors, which he distinguished from "motivator" factors in work (Herzberg, 1959). Institutional learning sanitizes and standardizes the learning environment, splitting the difference between the idiosyncracies of individual learners. It prescribes experiences and hopes that they will "take." It is a kind of defense against a fantasized anarchy in which everyone goes off in his or her own direction learning what he or she pleases. Such diversity of learning may—*may*—only be a problem from the point of view of someone who is supposedly responsible for the learning of a whole group of individuals—the typical school situation. But learning as a way of being does not presume a typical school situation and need not be defined by the norms and beliefs that have developed within that much more structured setting. And of course, learning as a way of being includes the idea that no one can be responsible for someone else's learning, any more than one person can be responsible for another person's consciousness.

Reflecting on the experiences of self-described successful learners thus teaches us a great deal about learning as a way of being. A second fruitful avenue along which to reflect on the nature of learning as a way of being is to ask people about *desired* learning experiences. What do they look and hope for in upcoming learning? A variation that yields even richer results is to ask people the following question (which grew out of my own experience as a parent as I noticed how angrily I would react to stories of arbitrary bureaucratic decisions being made by teachers and school administrators about my children's learning):

Think of someone whose learning you care a lot about, and suppose they are about to undergo a major learning experience. What characteristics would you want this experience to have for them?

The following twenty-six responses to this question were generated in 1992 by a group of twenty experienced human resource professionals. (Several subsequent repetitions of the survey have yielded very similar results. Where appropriate, I have noted the correspondence with one of more of the seven modes of learning as a way of being.)

- There is freedom to question, to disagree (self-directed, expressive, and reflexive learning).

- Learners have fun in the process (expressive and feeling learning).

- What is learned is reinforced (on-line and continual learning).

- The experience meets individuals' needs (self-directed, creative, expressive, and feeling learning).

- Participants use their own experiences to learn (on-line learning).

- The instructors have genuine concern for learners (feeling learning).

- Curiosity is encouraged and rewarded (self-directed, creative, expressive, continual, and reflexive learning).

- There is no doctrine of "one right way" present either in what or how to learn (self-directed, creative, and expressive learning).

- A nonjudgmental climate exists (feeling and reflexive learning).

- There is tolerance for mistakes (creative, expressive, and continual learning).

- There is acceptance of inherent knowledge and abilities (self-directed, creative, and on-line learning).

- Learners follow their inclinations (self-directed and creative learning).

- A nurturing environment exists (feeling and reflexive learning).

- There is tolerance of differences in learning styles (self-directed, creative, and feeling learning).

- A noncompetitive climate exists (expressive, feeling, and reflexive learning).

- The climate fosters creativity (creative and reflexive learning).

- The subject matter is interdisciplinary (creative and on-line learning).

- The concern is for attaining desired outcomes rather than merely for meeting norms (expressive, on-line, and reflexive learning).

- There is cultural diversity among learners (feeling, on-line, and reflexive learning).

- A variety of learning sources are used (creative, expressive, on-line, and reflexive learning).

- Genuine love and concern are present (feeling learning).

- Learners have time to reflect (self-directed and reflexive learning).

- Learners have an opportunity to teach (self-directed, creative, expressive, and reflexive learning).

- No one is made to feel stupid (feeling learning).

- The learning is self-paced (self-directed and continual learning).

- Everyone is stretched out of his or her comfort zone (creative, feeling, and reflexive learning).

Continual learning is the only mode of learning as a way of being that does not appear frequently in these descriptors, due probably to the way the question was asked. Yet clearly, these characteristics are important because they fit with natural inclinations of learners, and a learning process that has enough psychological validity to be comfortably sustained over an extended period of time is what continual learning is about. So I believe that continual learning is implied in these characteristics.

This is an impressive list of characteristics that the professionals I questioned would like to have present in the learning world of someone they care about. The institutional learning model can supply some but is antithetical to others. Moreover, it requires a designed environment, which is a far cry from permanent white water conditions. In white water, the learning process is continually buffeted by the same disruptions and emergencies that beset all organizations. Thus, that process has to incorporate an approach that can realize the desired characteristics whether they have been deliberately designed into the learning situation or not. In the exigencies and emergencies of white water, the learner has to be willing and able to direct his or her own learning process and to carry it out wherever he or she is at the time, not waiting for a more propitious time and place. Self-directed learning and on-line learning, in particular, will be important in this approach. And, in general, learning as a way of being is the means by which the learner will create his or her own felicitous learning world out of the resources that are available.

Conclusion

In closing this lengthy meditation on the nature of learning as a way of being, I stress once again the organic quality of learning as a way of being. It is, I have argued, an indispensable mode of conscious-ness for those of us who live in permanent white water. It is not a list of tips and techniques but a whole posture toward our experi-ence. Moreover, learning as a way of being is a naturally human way of being, indeed, its naturalness is its greatest asset. We must hope that our long experience of institutional learning has not beaten this natural consciousness totally out of us and that with a little encouragement and a few guiding ideas like the seven qualities pre-sented here, we may be able more fully to realize and to activate the wonderful learning capabilities that we all possess.

* * * * * * *

The next four chapters portray learning as a way of being in relation to four major areas of learning for the world of permanent white water. In reviewing the qualities of learning as a way of being, I have noted how the qualities interrelate. Learning as a way of being is a learning *system*, and reflexive learning is reflection on a *system* of events and experiences, not on six separate qualities of learning as a way of being. And it is systems learning as a way of being that is the first of the four major areas of learning that I will examine.

Part II

. . . .

Ways of Being

Strategies for Learning

3

· ·

Systems Learning

I am sitting in the back of the room as the next speaker in a week-long executive development program at a Fortune 50 company. The fifty participants are drawn from the top three echelons of the company. They are seated around tables for eight in the sunny top-floor conference room that anchors the company's state-of-the-art executive development complex. The present speaker is a well-known consultant and writer. He is taking the group through the basics of systems thinking as a prelude to a discussion of how systems thinking revolutionizes our understanding of top-level managerial leadership.[1] By any yardstick, the presentation is world class, both in content and delivery. All the systems basics are there, clearly and vigorously portrayed. But so too are the case illustrations, the humorous asides, and the passing brilliant commentaries on what can happen when a systems view is not taken. I, who thought I knew quite a bit about systems thinking, am fascinated, scribbling notes, excitedly planning how I can build on these ideas in my presentation that is yet to come. The participants, however, are reacting differently than I might have expected. The format is highly participative, and participation is not lacking, but its quality is troubling. Most of the questions and comments are skeptical

---

1.   This event occurred a few years prior to the appearance of Peter Senge's extra-ordinary presentation of systems thinking in *The Fifth Discipline* (1990).

and resistant. Many show a lack of understanding of the basic ideas that have been presented. There are mutterings of "too abstract" and "too complex" and "but will it work here?"

* * * * * * *

At the time this program took place, I was puzzled and even a little shocked by the reactions I heard. Why, I wondered, at this late date in the history of systems thinking should top managers in a large and well-managed company, which has a reputation for state-of-the-art innovations in management philosophy and practice, be having such a hard time with these simple ideas, especially when they were being so well presented? I felt these executives were not reacting any differently than their counterparts might have reacted forty years earlier.

Today, I have come to believe the culprit in such responses is institutional learning philosophy and practice. Systems thinking is paradigmatic of inappropriate subject matter for institutional learning structures and strictures. It is likely that organizations have been slow in establishing systems thinking because, first of all, institutional learning has taught us to think nonsystemically, and second, when systems thinking is presented through institutional learning filters, it loses most of its power and beauty.

Reflections on Systems Thinking

Thanks largely to Peter Senge's extraordinary book *The Fifth Discipline* (1990), *systems thinking* has become one of the most important bodies of ideas in the field of managerial leadership. Senge and others have made a compelling case for the nature of systems thinking and for its advantages in complex organizational situations. Now, the reality of permanent white water is an additional argument for systems thinking. The shocks and paradoxes of the turbulent situations with which we live and work cannot be eliminated, but perhaps they can be ameliorated with more powerful, comprehensive views of what they in fact are. Viewing these situations as *systems*, and coming to understand what that implies, is a promising approach and one I fully endorse.

Thus, the issue addressed in this chapter is not the nature of systems thinking and why systems thinking is a superior form of awareness. That I take as given. Rather, as is consistent with my overall theme, in this chapter I ask how systems thinking is *learned*. How well does the institutional learning model handle the subject matter called systems thinking? What if anything does learning as a way of being have to do with systems thinking? How can we improve the learning process for systems thinking?

Why are these questions important? The answer lies in the considerable evidence that systems thinking is not an easy form of consciousness and set of skills to acquire. The general notion of the importance of systems, knowledge of specific characteristics of systems, and the advantages of systems thinking as a frame of mind have been around for a good part of the twentieth century. Yet we continue to find ample evidence of absence of a systems awareness. We need look no further than to such common examples as the tendency to think in black-and-white, either-or terms; the tendency to believe in simple linear cause-effect relationships; the tendency to ignore feedback; the tendency to ignore the relationships between a phenomenon and its environment; the tendency to isolate a phenomenon in time, thus ignoring various time-based cycles; the tendency to ignore the natural boundaries of a phenomenon in favor of what we think its boundaries should be; and the tendency to believe that we can describe a phenomenon independently of ourselves as perceivers (that is, without considering systemic interactions between ourselves and the phenomenon). All of these examples are denials of a systems point of view, and we all commit them all the time—even those of us who are systems thinkers!

Because it reveals the shallowness and the fallacies in all the tendencies just mentioned, systems thinking is an enormously powerful frame of mind, but it is hardly ever comfortable or convenient in relation to our egocentric wishes. It complicates our world. It takes away our naïve beliefs in our power and control over things. It humbles our analytical abilities and bedevils us with complexities and imponderables that we would just as soon not bother with.

Calls to arms about systems thinking have been issued regularly for at least the last thirty years, really ever since von Bertalanffy's original work in the 1950s (von Bertalanffy, 1969). Kurt Lewin certainly thought in systems terms. His disciples Bennis, Benne, and Chin, in their book founding the field of organizational development (*The Planning of Change*, 1961), continually emphasize the systemic character of organizational phenomena. The famous "socio-technical systems" approach of the Tavistock Institute of Human Relations in London was thoroughly grounded in systems thinking (Emery, 1969). Russell Ackoff has consistently argued in his writings and many presentations for the superiority of a systems approach (Ackoff, 1974) and probably can be said to have exercised more vigorous leadership on behalf of systems thinking than any other individual. Indeed, his definition of a system has become virtually paradigmatic for management and organizations:

The elements of the set and the set of elements that form a system have the following three properties:

1. The properties or behavior of each element of the set has an effect on the properties or behavior of the set taken as a whole. For example, every organ in an animal's body affects its overall performance.
2. The properties and behavior of each element, and the way they affect the whole, depend on the properties and behavior of at least one other element in the set. Therefore, no part has an independent effect on the whole and each is affected by at least one other part. For example, the behavior of the heart and the effect it has on the body depend on the behavior of the lungs.

3. Every possible subgroup of elements in the set has the first two properties: each has a nonindependent effect on the whole. *Therefore, the whole cannot be decomposed into independent subsets. A system cannot be subdivided into independent subsystems.* For example, all of the subsystems in an animal's body—such as the nervous, respiratory, digestive, and motor subsystems—interact, and each affects the performance of the whole [1974, p. 13, emphasis added].

Katz and Kahn produced a very useful and widely read application of systems theory to organizations in the late 1960s (Katz and Kahn, 1966). Soon thereafter, "the systems approach" began to be used as a cornerstone organizing idea in mainstream management textbooks, of which one of the first was Kast and Rosenweig (1969).

It is not as well known as it should be that the Elton Mayo–Fritz Roethlisberger group at the Harvard Business School was committed to a version of systems thinking from the late 1930s onward. Roethlisberger and Dickson's famous theory chapter in *Management and the Worker* (1939, chap. 24) is called "The Industrial Organization as a Social System" and contains many statements that embody a systems view. In a little-known but important later statement, Roethlisberger stressed the need for learners to understand "part-whole relationships" (the same relationships defined by Ackoff) (Roethlisberger, Lombard, and Ronken, 1954, p. 143). Mayo and Roethlisberger had been influenced by Lawrence J. Henderson who, as a physician-professor in the Harvard Medical School, transferred his knowledge of systems properties of biological phenomena over to his interest in the well-known Hawthorne studies that Mayo and Roethlisberger were conducting at the Chicago Hawthorne Plant of Western Electric (Barber, 1970). Henderson in turn was influenced by Walter Cannon's *The Wisdom of the Body*, in which the very systems-oriented notion of homeostasis was first developed (Cannon, 1939), and by the writings of the great nineteenth-century physiologist Claude Bernard, whose ideas about how the systemic nature of phenomena influences the way one should go about investigating them and experimenting on them can still be read with profit today by those interested in studying human systems (Bernard, [1927] 1949). Henderson also influenced Chester Barnard, author of *The Functions of the Executive* (1938), a book filled with systems thinking, and George Homans, who employed systems thinking in his landmark study *The Human Group* (1950).

Mayo and Roethlisberger found additional support for systems approaches to human organizations in the anthropological writings of such researchers as A. R. Radcliffe-Brown (1957) and Bronislaw Malinowski (1944). When one does not understand a phenomenon *at all*, as an anthropologist coming new to a society may not, a systems approach is indispensable. Otherwise, the alien sights and sounds are a hopelessly swirling jumble. One does not know what to pay attention to nor how anything is connected to anything else. A systems approach at least helps an investigator understand that the problem is to discover the underlying connections and interdependencies.

There are of course many other writers and schools of thought that could be mentioned were I compiling a comprehensive history of the systems idea as it has come to be applied to human organizations. On the contemporary scene, chaos theory, which is receiving so much attention now, is not antithetical to systems thinking. In fact, one might say that what chaos theory tries to do is discover systemic relationships among phenomena that are apparently behaving randomly and unpredictably.

Drawing on Ackoff's definition, it seems that the core idea of systems thinking is the balancing and interrelating of three levels of phenomena: first, the *thing-of-interest* (or *whole*, or *phenomenon*) be it an organization, a personality, a piece of protoplasm, or a solar system; second, the inner workings of the thing-of-interest, the combining and interacting of the internal elements to produce— in some way that is not just linear and additive—the thing-of-interest; and third, the world outside the thing-of-interest and the connections and interactions of the thing-of-interest with that world, that is, the phenomenon in its context. Systems thinking also requires that we view the phenomenon and its surrounding world as moving dynamically in time.

The Distinctive Problems of Learning Systems Thinking

Systems thinking asks its practitioner to embrace complexity, contingency, dynamism, and perhaps even mystery. In the world of permanent white water, we can understand why a managerial leader might be instinctively uneasy about a mode of thinking that takes him or her so thoroughly out of his or her comfort zone, a mode of thinking that may seem to exacerbate turbulence, to create white water of the mind. Systems thinking is not a reductionistic task through which we search for the one or two factors that "explain" a phenomenon. Instead, systems thinking asks its practitioner *simultaneously* to hold the whole in mind *and* to investigate the interactions of the component elements of the whole—all the component elements, not just the two or three most obvious and easy to examine— *and* to investigate the relation of the whole to its larger environment.

There are three things in particular about systems thinking that deserve special mention as learning challenges. One is that because a system is open to its environment, as all human systems are, and because all its internal elements influence each other and the whole in complex and often unpredictable ways, a systems thinker can never know everything there is to know about a system. An open system forever transcends complete understanding. Systems thinking immerses the thinker in a process of ongoing inquiry. *Systems thinking, therefore, is continual learning. Because of the very nature of systems, it cannot be anything else.*

Second, managerial leaders are deeply involved members of the organizations they are trying to understand as social systems. How an inquirer participates in the phenomena he or she is examining has received major attention recently from Wheatley (1992). The idea of participation and connectedness between observer and observed is an old and controversial one in the social sciences, chiefly because the objectivism that has dominated social science seems so much simpler to learn and to practice (Truzzi, 1974; Barfield, [1957] 1977). Nevertheless, inquiry into a social system alters its dynamics and has an impact back on the inquirer, so that our inquiry delves into ourselves and our relation to the system as much as into the system itself. *Learning systems thinking, therefore, is learning about oneself in interaction with the surrounding world.* We do not so much learn *about* a system as we learn in, through, and of a system.

Finally, systems thinking is content-free in its essentials. It is a little like statistics in this regard, although in statistics, the concepts and terms at least relate to each other mathematically. In systems thinking, we cannot be sure of what we are learning and what we have to talk about until all the abstract jargon and all the propositions about systems have been brought to bear on some real thing in the real world. Even concrete examples of various systems ideas may be inadequate to clinch the power of the basic notions for the learner. Learning systems thinking can therefore be very frustrating. In a literal sense, learners may feel they do not know what they are talking about.

For these three reasons in particular, learning systems thinking is a challenge. Perhaps these reasons also explain why systems thinking has not long since become a common and standardized way to approach any phenomenon. Why indeed isn't all learning systems thinking and learning? The systems model presumably applies to any thing-of-interest, from building a model airplane to learning a foreign language to conducting a policy analysis of a new piece of legislation. In principle, all learning is systems learning. It is all the more ironic, then, that this way of thinking should continue to be in its infancy in the extent to which it has penetrated the popular consciousness.

In particular, we may wonder whether the institutional learning model could survive if we really understood phenomena as systems. Many of the standard practices of institutional learning assume that the subject matter is not a system, that the learner is not a system, that an instructor and a group of learners are not a social system, that the instructor is not systemically connected to other instructors and to the subject matter, and ultimately, that the learning process through which all these systems combine and interact is not a system. Institutional learning practices dis-integrate subject matter and dis-integrate learners in order to package and schedule subject matter and learners at the institution's convenience. It is profoundly ironic that in the formal education of managerial leaders, some of this subject matter professes to discuss "systems thinking." It even might be scheduled as a "learning module." And right there, in the frequent use of that phrase, is the antisystems bias of the institutional learning model. That model does not want everything to be connected to everything else, because the more connections that are admitted to be of importance, the more challenging it is to teach the material.

Learning as a Way of Being and Systems Thinking

In the previous chapter, I described the self-reported learning processes of successful learners. What is fairly obvious from the way these people talked about their learning is that the process of becoming increasingly competent amounts to an increasing understanding of a subject in what can be called systems terms. Whatever it is they have become good at is not fragmented for them, not isolated from its environment, not isolated in time or in space. They know the relevant elements and their interrelations intimately. These learners have a feeling for the *meaning* of the subject beyond its technical details and its formal structure. They have *operative* knowledge about this system, which is to say they know how to get this complex something to work in the way they intend, whether that something be carving a piece of wood or debugging a computer program or engaging in productive dialogue with another person (the system here, of course, is the dialogue process, not the other person).

If successful learning both embodies learning as a way of being and leads the learner toward an increasingly systemic understanding of a thing-of-interest, we may conclude, tentatively, that the practice of learning as a way of being *produces* systems thinking. It is in prescribing the converse situation that the institutional learning model may betray the teacher of systems thinking. The institutional learning model wants the teacher to talk *about* systems thinking, not to coach the practice of it. Whereas a person learning about a system by engaging in learning as a way of being will keep the conceptual superstructure of systems thinking to a minimum in favor of immersion in the phenomenon that he or she is trying to understand in systems terms.

Let me push the argument of the last few paragraphs one further step—to its logical conclusion: systems thinking can probably not be taught or learned effectively within a learning philosophy that is itself profoundly antisystemic. (Ackoff, 1974, appears to have come to the same conclusion. He is, at least, quite clear that his key concept of "interactive planning" cannot be learned let alone practiced through traditional classroom instruction.) Certainly no one would try to teach a foreign language without letting the students practice speaking it. How can we teach systems thinking in bits and pieces? It is a self-contradictory proposition. Learning as a way of being, however, is a promising philosophy by which to learn systems thinking.

Indeed, I suggest that learning as a way of being is prerequisite to learning systems thinking. Learning as a way of being is itself a system of ideas about learning and experiences of learning. It involves the learner in real time (on-line and continual learning). It preserves the wholeness of subject matter by freeing the learner to explore that wholeness, relatively unrestrained by "proper" ways to approach the material (self-directed, creative, and expressive learning). It encourages the learner in personal ways of knowing that are meaningful for that person (expressive learning and felt meaning). It asks the learner to let the learning process keep affecting itself and the course of future learning (reflexive learning).

Ackoff's three characteristics of a system apply to the seven qualities of learning as a way of being itself: (1) each of the seven contributes to the overall effect of learning as a way of being; (2) no one of the seven qualities is truly independent of the others; (3) any subgroups of two or three remain in systemic relationships with each other and with the whole. Tempting as it may be, we cannot take just one or two of the qualities, perhaps those that may seem easiest to implement, and hope to get the benefits of learning as a way of being by focusing on just these elements. Experiential learning in the institutional learning model focuses on expressive learning, for example, but by ignoring some of the other qualities, especially self-directed and reflexive learning, many learners do not get the point of the expressiveness they are encouraged to engage in. Other educators place great emphasis on reflexive learning while otherwise practicing the institutional learning philosophy. But reflexive learning is impoverished for a learner who has no personal stake in the subject matter (no self-directed learning) and has little opportunity to experiment with it (no creative or expressive learning) and to feel its meaning (no feeling learning). Without the other six qualities, reflexive learning is, as learners might say, navel gazing.

Systems Learning as a Way of Being

What are some approaches to learning that might be more supportive of a systems point of view, that might help the learner consciously learn to think systemically even as he or she is learning some body of subject matter? This is a fundamental question. It seems to happen by default with successful learners. But could it be more deliberately fostered if we could free ourselves, relatively at least, from the strictures of the institutional learning philosophy? I think the answer is yes, and I offer below some beginning ideas that have promise. The main message of this final section, however, is that we urgently need to develop many more learning philosophies and methods that are more appropriate to gaining an understanding of systems. Learning as a way of being is one such approach. But beyond learning as a way of being, perhaps systems thinking is the very "subject matter" that might force much broader reconsideration of the limitations of institutional learning philosophy. If Senge and his colleagues' emphasis on systems thinking continues to take hold and capture the attention and the imagination of managerial leaders, it will require change of historic proportions in the organizational systems we use to conduct learning.

In the remainder of this chapter, I discuss one broad set of approaches to learning systems thinking. While they appear close to an already well-established tradition in management education—namely, the so-called case method of instruction—I hasten to add that what I make of these case-oriented approaches is quite different from popular stereotypes of the case method.

The case method was originally adopted at the Harvard Business School in 1908 because the Harvard Law School had had such success with "classroom discussion of practical problems" (McNair, 1954, p. 25). Within a few years, however, it gradually became clear that case method instruction was an approach to learning that could accomplish things in other fields that principle-oriented lecturing could not accomplish. The nature of the resulting learning was captured in Gragg's memorable phrase of justification, "because wisdom can't be told" (McNair, 1954).

The original case method has been the subject of many subsequent modifications and innovations. This is not the place to chronicle that method's history and its present pedagogical status. Just one point is crucial to a discussion of improved methods of systems learning. The case method focuses the learner's attention on the *whole* as it manifests itself in organizational reality. The case method puts the learner, almost unconsciously, in a position where systems thinking can operate: a case can portray a whole office, a whole plant, a whole industry, a whole product development cycle, a whole career development process, and so on. Even when a case does not contain all the information a learner would want, it gets the learner thinking about the whole picture as it concretely exists, and this is the crucial prerequisite to systems thinking.

In terms of learning as a way of being, it is an interesting exercise to reflect on how the case method of instruction does or does not foster one or another of the qualities of learning as a way of being. Such reflection will show that a great deal depends on the way cases are used in a curriculum, how committed a school is to the approach, and the extent to which instructors have found ways of supporting learning as a way of being qualities in the way they present cases.

However, there is one deficiency in the classic case approach that is difficult to overcome: the learner is presented with the case. It is a prestructured situation. The learner has not decided what data to include, what to highlight, and what to give subordinate emphasis. The learner has not decided what the case is *about*. Most importantly, the case is probably not about a system that is of any personal interest to the learner. The learner has not chosen the industry or company of the case nor the particular managerial situation it portrays. This is not to say learners do not become interested in one case or another, but it is a derivative interest, an interest that arises elsewhere than in the learner's own curiosity and motivation. Thus, the case method risks the loss of both self-directed learning and creative learning because it discourages the learner from thinking of the case data as his or her own, produced and structured by his or her own efforts.

As every case researcher and writer knows, a case can be collected and written in an almost infinite number of ways. The system that is to become the case is not merely *there*, waiting to be realistically "photographed" by an observer. Case research and writing is a consciously directed stream of decisions about the meaning of the data and their role in the overall case. A case is sculpted by a case researcher and writer from the first hour of his or her contact with the source of the data. Case research and writing is, furthermore, an iterative and interactive stream of decisions as the case researcher and writer interacts with case characters and with his or her own supervisors, sees the case used on a trial basis with students, and reflects on all the decisions that have been made to produce the case.

All of which is to say that case research and writing utilizes a far greater range and depth of learning as a way of being qualities than does analysis of a case someone else has written. If we truly want learners to learn systems thinking we will help them become case researchers and writers. Case research forces the investigator to wonder, "What is related to what?"—to wonder about connectedness and about causality. The investigator discovers that system "elements" are not conveniently scattered about, like jigsaw pieces waiting to be assembled into the "right" picture. A system element is an abstraction deduced from the flow of events in the system. The right way to frame the elements and their interrelations is never exactly clear, and an investigator is unlikely to forget how much a particular configuration is his or her own. Conversely, how much of themselves people put into their descriptions of the systems that they examine cannot be learned by reading their descriptions of the systems.

There is one other insight into the case researcher and writer's mentality that is indispensable. He or she is researching and writing for a purpose; the process is not one of aimless osmosis. But neither is the case researcher just testing a preformed hypothesis. He or she is both open to all the exigencies of the situation *and* aware of the need to bring them into some kind of a coherent pattern that will have learning value for someone else. This mentality is strikingly similar to that required of a managerial leader, and it is the person who aspires to be a managerial leader whom we are seeking to help learn to think in systems terms.

The learning of the case researcher is relatively free of institutional learning practices (although, predictably, there are constant pressures and temptations to find a repeatable formula for case research and writing). Case research and writing is learning as a way of being, and the process is the researcher's immersion in systems thinking, whether it is called that or not.

Systems Learning in Human Systems

Modern systems thinking was not developed with human organizations and other groupings as the phenomena of interest. Physical and nonhuman biological systems were the initial settings in which systems ideas were developed. But suppose someone had told the early systems thinkers three things about the phenomena they were trying to understand in systems terms—three things that are characteristic of all human beings singly and in groups?

1. Your phenomena have the *essential* property of being able to generate new states in themselves (think new thoughts, do new things) that they have never manifested before. Indeed, they are best thought of as continually *trying* to generate such new states.

2. Your phenomena have the property of being able to notice your attempts to theorize about them and model them, and they modify themselves according to their reaction to this information.

3. A key characteristic of your phenomena is that they make a continuing stream of conscious and unconscious value judgments about their experiences. As you are a member yourself of this class of phenomena, you will find it impossible to refrain from making value judgments about other members of the class. All your theories and models, therefore, will not be purely descriptive but will incorporate your own values, feelings, and imperfections, *no matter how hard you try to eliminate them.*

The first proposition can be called creativity; the second, reactivity; and the third, participation. So to these early systems thinkers, someone could have said, "Your 'system' is creative, it is reactive to your analysis of it, and you cannot avoid participating in it." What would systems thinking look like today if the early systems thinkers, from the outset, had thought of their phenomena in these terms: in terms of unpredictability rather than predictability and in terms of continuous interaction with all observers rather than of detachment and objectivity, that is, in terms of themselves as parts of the systems they were modelling?

While we cannot predict with absolute certainty what systems thinking would be like today had its founders worked with images of human rather than nonhuman systems, we can speculate that our methods for learning systems thinking might be quite different. In particular, I suggest that we might have learned to pay more attention to methodologies already at hand for studying human groupings in systems terms, although we currently do not think of them as tools for understanding systems. These methodologies are novels and poems, plays and films—ways of peering into the complexities and mysteries of human beings singly and in groupings. They are readily available. Each genre has an extensive tradition and literature. Each, in fact, probably has its own problems with institutional learning. But maybe systems learning as a way of being needs to take another look at these methods for the learning potential they contain (Burden, 1988; Puffer, 1991).

Conclusion

Reflection on the problems that have prevented the widespread adoption of systems thinking indicates that learning systems thinking probably cannot be done very well when constrained by the institutional learning philosophy. The only way to learn systems thinking is to break out of institutional learning practices into a learning process that is more involving, presents more complexity, and requires the learner to think in systems terms in the real time of learning. Case research and writing is one type of activity that does exactly these things.

More broadly, the search should be on for other methods of immersing learners in purposeful wholes (which are what all human systems are) and allowing learners to pursue their own systems learning within these purposeful wholes. If we are serious about producing systems thinkers, we have to take the need for methods of systems learning more seriously. In any such additional methods, the learner's own reflections (reflexive learning) must be the primary source of the *general* knowledge about systems per se that systems thinkers have always insisted is so important.

✦ ✦ ✦ ✦ ✦ ✦ ✦

The basic reason systems learning is so important, beyond its intrinsic delights, is its value to managerial leaders as they think about how to lead and manage groupings of people. I have not talked much in this chapter about action taking, about making things happen in organizations. That is the task of leadership, and the next chapter takes up the nature of leadership in the world of permanent white water and the importance of learning as a way of being to leaders in that world.

4

· ·

Leaderly Learning

T his chapter takes up leadership as the second of four broad topics that illustrate the dynamics of learning as a way of being.
With all that has been said about leadership in recent years, particularly the extraordinary outpouring of ideas about visionary and
charismatic leadership, we might wonder whether there is anything
left to be said. Indeed, we might wearily wonder whether there is
anything left to be said as the theories proliferate about what it is
that leaders do, what the critical qualities of character in leaders
are, what "competencies" leaders possess, and how these can be
imparted in education and training. Haven't we said enough about
leadership? Why don't we just take what we have and spend our
energy helping contemporary leaders and trying to increase the
number of younger men and women who learn these ideas?

Well, no matter how numbing all this work may be, we know the
leadership field is not going to shrivel. Leadership theory and research
will continue to be a growth industry, and to be fair, there continue
to be plenty of fascinating questions we can ask about leadership, particularly now that both genders as well as individuals from a diversity
of cultures are getting involved in the practice of modern theories of
managerial leadership. (For example, one particularly interesting new
approach is that of Drath and Paulus, 1994, who argue that leadership is not the behavior of a person at all but rather a property of a
social system or, as they call it, a "community of practice" [p. 11].)

It is also the case that methods of educating and training leaders will continue to develop. Yet institutional learning philosophy still dominates leadership education, and as I have been illustrating in these pages, the undervaluing of learning as a way of being in the institutional learning model is particularly apparent in today's education for managerial leadership. Even though there are also plenty of so-called experiential educational methods around (see, for example, any issue of the *Journal of Management Education*), reading about leadership and listening to experts talk about leadership are still the dominant educational modes in our nation's business schools and corporate training programs. But experiential learning according to institutional learning principles has a circumscribed meaning: experts decide what learnings learners need; experiences are then designed for learners so that they all will have the same experiences at the same time and same place and from the same teaching material and can then be graded on their attainment of the principles and practices. Institutional learning is not particularly interested in learners' own experiences as leaders. And it definitely does not encourage learners to reflect on what is involved in learning leadership, that is, in what might be called *leaderly learning*. Thus, over the years, the institutional learning model has undercut the intended spirit of experiential learning. It has lost its learner-centered quality and its core commitment to learner experimentation with learning experiences.

Three Deans a-Learning

Let me introduce the main point of this chapter by recounting an unusual opportunity I have had to observe managerial leadership. In 1973, I joined what was then called the School of Government and Business Administration of my university as dean of the school. I held this position for the next five years and then resigned because I thought the school needed a different kind of dean for the challenges that lay ahead. Rather than leave the school, however, I stayed on the faculty as a professor and have held that position ever since. In the succeeding seventeen years, three other individuals have occupied the deanship. It is highly unusual to have the opportunity to observe firsthand one, let alone three, senior executives' performance of a job that one understands intimately oneself. The relatively collegial environment of academe made my opportunity to do so possible and legitimate.

The role of dean is a classic upper-middle manager role, like the division general manager role in industry. Deans are like colonels in the army or bureau chiefs in government. Their role is unique, however, in that while its scope of responsibility is wide, it is much more limited in authority than positions of comparable responsibility in other organizations. The reason for this is the collegial form of government practiced in higher education. A dean has to consult the faculty on practically everything he or she does. The faculty then deliberate, sometimes in committees, sometimes in a general body, sometimes in small ad hoc groupings. The dean's ideas and opinions about mission and objectives; about curriculum; about organization structure; about appointment, promotion, and retention of faculty; about space allocation; about public ceremonies such as commencement; and about many other things as well all receive the faculty's individual and collective scrutiny. Even in areas where a dean thinks he or she has a relatively free hand, if faculty decide they should have a voice on a particular decision a wise dean will usually accede to the demand. (Although, as most deans ruefully have learned, there is one area in which faculty members rarely demand a voice and opportunity to participate. That area is fundraising.) Relative to his or her counterparts in business, therefore, an academic dean has always been more a reflector or amplifier of faculty opinion than a source of top-down leadership. The performance pressure on a dean is probably not as intense as it is on upper-middle managers in modern business, but in all other respects, the job is as difficult and demanding as in any other organization.

It is not false modesty for me to say that all three of my successors had much more experience as organizational leaders than I had when they took on this position of great responsibility but rather less authority. All three had excellent qualifications for the position, having occupied executive positions of substantial authority and responsibility in industry, government, and the military as well as in higher education. All three were more than twenty years older when they assumed the position than I had been in 1973. In addition, two knew the academic culture well while the third, though lacking direct academic experience, had a great deal of leadership experience in corporate training and development and had represented his firm and his industry in committee work with the American Assembly of Collegiate Schools of Business, the main accrediting agency for business schools. All three had a leadership style that was compatible with academic culture. In addition to their practical experience, all three had a well-developed conceptual understanding of organizational leadership and of current theories and trends about leadership. Two of the three had a wide circle of friends and uniform respect among the school faculty, having been professors there before becoming deans, and both had previously performed other leadership positions of substantial scope in the school.

As with any executive role, many things can be said about the key requirements of being an effective dean. The production of general statements about what it takes to be effective as a top manager is one of the leading academic growth industries. However, I have not seen much if any emphasis on one of the most obvious and constant characteristics of the way my three successor deans did the job. For all three individuals, the deanship was a nonstop learning process. Week after week and year after year, I could point to some pending issue or some process being initiated that was relatively novel and untried and for which there was no formula; there were various players who had various ideas about what ought to be done; there was action that was time sensitive relative to the academic calendar, and failure to act would mean loss of as much as a year on whatever the issue was; and frequently there was an issue that involved the technicalities of one academic specialty or another that the dean might at best only vaguely understand. The seventeen-year period was also marked by extraordinary ferment in higher education generally on such issues as the tightening and streamlining of management practices, the future of academic tenure, the changing of accreditation standards, the drying up of traditional sources of external funding, the increase in government regulation, the complexities and uncertainties of developing studies abroad and programs with an international focus, and the detaching of education from the bricks and mortar of campuses and classrooms.

Moreover, because of the constant presence of white water, such strategic issues as these cannot be matters of calm deliberation. There is a continuing stream of interruptions and aberrations that demand attention: unexpected faculty conflicts, snits, and resignations; lawsuits, actual and threatened; student high jinks and protests; unannounced arrivals of visiting dignitaries from all over the world; random requests and proposals from well-meaning alumni and parents; foreign students stranded with no money; allegations of cheating and other improprieties among both students and faculty; and the like—all matters that soak up great chunks of a dean's time. The first thing a dean learns is how much in a school gets delegated upward to the dean's office because no one else knows what to do about it or sometimes even cares. Doubtless general managers in other organizations have discovered this same pattern.

No one knew *the* answer on any of these issues, neither the answer to the substantive strategic question nor to the surprising, novel, messy, obtrusive events that are the permanent white water. Everyone was on a steep learning curve and remained so. Leaderly learning was occurring for my successor deans on all these issues and more. I do not know if they defined their jobs primarily as nonstop learning processes. I know that I did not during my tenure. From time to time, when our struggle to get on top of some issue has been unusually stimulating and/or exhausting, most of us have probably ruefully muttered something about the situation's being "a real learning experience," but our institutional learning has not taught us to frame something like the role of a dean as *primarily* a learning experience. Instead, it has kept us focused on the doing/performing/achieving ways of framing an executive role. Institutional learning is preliminary and ancillary to the main characteristic of that role, which is to get things done.

When we are preoccupied with getting things done, it suppresses our attention to our own learning. An observer can see that—as I have been able to do with my three successors—but it is not something the three deans have been able to be too open about themselves. It is not easy in our culture for a leader to admit that he or she feels like a learner. As I discussed earlier, in the philosophy of institutional learning, to be a learner is to be incompetent. To be incompetent, the logic continues, is to be unqualified for the position. At best, a dean or other new executive is allowed a "honeymoon," during which time he or she is allowed to be a learner, that is, to make mistakes, ask "dumb" questions, be unclear on priorities, and so forth. But when the honeymoon is over, the culture of the typical organization requires that the executive exude confidence and clarity. Whatever learning is still going on is driven underground, out of sight of associates and maybe even out of the awareness of the executive.

Leaderly Learning

The main hypothesis of this chapter is that *managerial leadership is not learned; managerial leadership is learning*. Permanent white water has made learning the preeminent requirement of all managerial leadership, beyond all the other characteristics and requisite competencies.

Institutional learning philosophy assumes that managerial leadership is something that can be learned and sets out to teach it, whether in a university classroom, a sumptuous corporate training center, or a rough-and-ready "ropes course" in the back country. Institutional learning philosophy has implanted in our culture and deep in our ways of looking at ourselves the idea that managerial leadership can be learned like any other subject. So, at substantial physical, psychological, and financial cost, thousands on thousands of learners are earnestly trying to learn it. They, and their teachers, are making a mistake: managerial leadership is not learned; it is learning. Managerial leadership is a powerful form of learning as a way of being.

I have given this form of learning as a way of being a special name: *leaderly learning*. The word *learning* is not used here as a noun, meaning "knowledge attained." Rather it is to be taken as a gerund— thus, it describes an ongoing process of action. The ongoing process of learning is occurring all the time in executive life. The word *leaderly* is an adjective modifying learning. Thus, *leaderly learning* is the kind of learning that a managerial leader needs to engage in as an ongoing process in the job.

The premise that managerial leadership *is* leaderly learning I call the *learning premise*. When an individual applies the learning premise to himself or herself and becomes comfortable with it, it changes everything. It puts a managerial leader in a completely different frame of mind than he or she had once accepted as natural. The kind and quality and degree of learning going on in the managerial leader and in others become primary criteria for describing and evaluating any situation. The meaning of the managerial leader's responsibilities is altered. His or her relationships to colleagues are altered, especially team relationships. The evaluation criteria the managerial leader uses and would prefer that others use are altered. The human meaning of his or her work and of its consequences for others are altered. He or she becomes more self-accepting and less concerned about perfection in the frustrating white water conditions. Most of all, once the managerial leader accepts the learning premise, what he or she does with time allotted to formal education and training experiences is altered. No longer can formal education and training be what it now is—a literally manic process of fearfully cramming large amounts of technical material into the brain in hopes that enough will be retained to be useful when it is needed. No longer can institutional learning philosophy and practice dominate the managerial leader's learning process. This philosophy and practice does not prepare a person for a role that is primarily continual learning before it is anything else. This philosophy and practice does not create in a person the capacity to practice learning as a way of being.

Then, if managerial leadership is leaderly learning, formal education for such work becomes learning about leaderly learning itself—discovering the kind of learning that managerial leaders, like the three deans, must continually engage in.

Learning about leaderly learning is a crucial but elusive element of my argument and of my repeated criticism of institutional learning for teaching us little about our own learning processes. If managerial leadership *is* leaderly learning, it means that persons in these leadership jobs need to understand the varieties of leaderly learning, the strengths and weaknesses of various methods of leaderly learning, the organizational conditions that aid or hinder leaderly learning, the variations in leaderly learning styles, and the like. If leaderly learning is the crucial ability in effective white water managerial leadership, it becomes essential that would-be managerial leaders understand more about it. Rather than devoting all their time in formal education and training to receiving imparted facts and methods *about* a subject, would-be managerial leaders should have the opportunity in these formal settings to learn about leaderly learning. Instead of memorizing "subject matter," would-be managerial leaders can learn about learning processes in general by becoming immersed in the seven qualities of learning as a way of being.

In addition, every subject poses its own learning challenges. If I know that for the rest of my professional life I am going to be learning about new ways to organize, manage, and lead human beings, for example, what can I learn during a period of formal education about the special learning problems presented by new material on human behavior in organizations? If I know I am going to be learning about computerized systems, both hardware and software, for the rest of my professional life, what do I need to learn now about the special learning problems presented by computer systems? If I know I am going to be learning about new kinds of financial instruments for the rest of my professional life, what can I learn now about the special learning problems presented by financial instruments?

What I focus on will not be exclusively learning processes, of course. To understand the learning challenges of financial instruments, we have to talk about financial instruments; we have to acquire technical knowledge about them. But the learning premise says that the way I go about my beginning encounter with the mysterious world of financial instruments is crucial. If I practice the approach in which subject matter is impersonal technical facts to be memorized and regurgitated in a sheltered off-line environment, in intense competition for grades with other learners, and with an instructor practicing essentially one-way communication in a god-like expert posture—and if while all this happens any discussion of my own learning processes for such material is merely tacit, I will not have been preparing myself very well to continue to learn about financial instruments for the rest of my career.

Special Problems in Learning About Human Behavior in Organizations

All subject matter areas relevant to managerial leaders need to be examined for their special learning problems. For example, take the area of learning new ways to organize, manage, and lead human beings, and ask, What might we like a learner to know about the learning challenges of this continuing stream of new ideas, so that he or she can engage in that kind of leaderly learning more effectively over the course of a career? In the years that I have been working with would-be managerial leaders on the subject of human behavior in organizations, I have discovered that the following seven learning challenges arise repeatedly.

- First, in order to grasp new ideas about human behavior in organizations, we must learn how to surface and examine our assumptions about human beings—assumptions that derive from our past experiences and also assumptions that are built into any specific principles we have already been employing. The assumptions we make about human behavior help us hold our world steady, help us give order and meaning to our world, and therefore have profound psychological significance. To question our assumptions is to shake up our world, filling us with pain and anxiety. Managerial leaders need to learn early the importance of questioning assumptions and methods for doing it.

- Second, the subject matter for learning about human behavior in organizations is a rather confusing mixture of findings from the empirical research of behavioral science, traditional common sense, and an intermediate body of quasi-scientific theories and hunches that are richly suggestive but possibly of questionable validity. Material about human behavior in organizations poses serious epistemological problems in other words, and if the learner is not aware of the need to ask questions about how material came to be known and how much is really known, it is possible to seriously under- or overestimate the value of any particular concept or interpretation. (I once gave a group of doctoral students a list of twenty or so common fallacies in reasoning and asked the group to examine the first chapter of a top-selling management book of the 1980s and 1990s for examples. No one got more than a few pages into the first chapter because practically every sentence employed one or more fallacies. That thousands of organizations were energetically trying to implement the principles the book espoused put the students into a state of acute cognitive dissonance.)

- A third challenge, which follows from the epistemological problems defined in the second challenge, is to achieve a personal synthesis about human behavior in organizations that balances and integrates all the kinds of data and concepts that are available. The huge variety of material available will not be usable if it merely resides in the learner's mind as a collection of possible ways of talking about human behavior in organizations. However, the synthesis or framework also cannot go to the other extreme and become fixed dogma in the learner's mind.

• Fourth, a managerial leader presumably has a strong action focus, a concern for getting things done. It is not easy to maintain an action focus when there are so many intriguing ways of talking about human behavior in organizations. The learner needs to discover and recognize the temptations to become a passive speculator and contemplator or a detached critic and skeptic. Neither posture is the frame of mind a managerial leader needs to be in.

• Part of achieving an action focus as a managerial leader is achieving a balance between objectivity and subjectivity, between one's personal perspective—reflecting individual values and priorities—and a more impersonal, objective stance that takes account of other points of view in a situation. This is a fifth tension created by the subject matter of human behavior in organizations that learners need to understand.

• Sixth, material about human behavior in organizations exists on a continuum from the deep intrapersonal to the macrosociological. Different learners will have different tastes in and reactions to issues at various points along the continuum. Some will enjoy the micro and be bored with the macro; others will reverse these responses. Managerial leaders, however, need the capacity to range with understanding across the entire spectrum, from the details of one person's motivation to how several thousand people might react to a new policy.

• Finally, a major consequence of learning material about human behavior in organizations should be to grasp the huge variety of contexts to which the basic ideas can be applied. In our thoroughly organizational world, material on human behavior in organizations relates to much more than a person's formal career as a managerial leader. The study of human behavior in organizations has the potential to change our consciousness about all areas of experience and in relation to all the different organizations we have contact with in any capacity. Beginners in the subject often find that ideas about human behavior in organizations illuminate their family and romantic relationships. They also find the ideas relevant to their experiences as clients and customers of organizations. If we permit it, lifelong learning about human behavior in organizations will affect what we know in all categories of experience.

Learning about human behavior in organizations will be different for the learner who is helped to understand these seven learning challenges than it is for the learner who takes the subject at face value and is unaware of and unprepared for some of its challenging and transforming effects. The former learner is becoming much better prepared for *lifelong* leaderly learning.

I have used human behavior in organizations as the example here not because I think it is particularly special but simply because it is the subject on which I am best qualified to illustrate the process of identifying learning challenges. I think that the same kind of analysis I have applied to the subject of human behavior in organizations can and should be made for all the subjects that are necessary to leaderly learning.

Many educators have noted the particular learning challenges of their own specialties. Presumably, that is what a good teacher is good at—anticipating the kinds of problems learners are going to have with specific material. The next step, as counseled by institutional learning philosophy, however, is simply to design the presentation of that material with these problems in mind, without insisting that the learners *themselves* acquire insight into the learning challenges and into the various options that exist for meeting them. So far as I am aware, not many educators know how to design their presentations, courses, workshops, textbooks, and the like in such a way as to (1) enhance a learner's understanding of the learning challenges posed by the material, and (2) prepare the learner for a learning process of indefinite duration for meeting these learning challenges. What we need in education for managerial leadership is a thorough review of the learning challenges of leaderly learning. We should then follow that by working out a process for helping learners come to understand these learning challenges.

Toward a Program for Leaderly Learning

The following discussion is not intended to be definitive but illustrative. My basic intent is to make the case for a long-term reform in the way we are educating men and women for managerial leadership. And—mea culpa!—I include myself as I call into question the work of virtually all those who have been, so they thought, teaching managerial leadership.

Our current education for managerial leadership is much too subject-matter oriented. Curricula, whether in higher education or corporate training and development, are dominated by an obsession with teaching learners what leaders need to know. In the last chapter, I noted that systems thinking is antithetical to institutional learning philosophy and practice. We cannot learn systems thinking well as long as we regard it through the institutional learning lens. The same can be said about managerial leadership. I have argued elsewhere that managerial leadership is a *performing* art (Vaill, 1989a) and that we are not teaching learners very much at all about *running* an organization (Vaill, 1992).

Looking at leaderly learning through a different lens, that of the seven qualities of learning as a way of being, permits me to say much more about what learning leaderly learning needs to be like, bearing in mind that the learner must be engaged in a continual learning process for the rest of his or her career. After showing how learning as a way of being helps us understand leaderly learning, I will describe a few generic learning problems for managerial leaders.

Self-Directed Leaderly Learning

It is seemingly often forgotten in scholarly discussions about leadership that before it is anything else, leadership is *initiative*. Why else use the word *leader* in leadership? It stands to reason that a powerful force supporting a person's initiating (leading) is the experience and feeling of having personally directed the learning process that is resulting in the decision to exercise initiative. This experience and feeling is self-directed learning. The person taking initiative is thinking through (learning) what is needed and why. He or she is thinking through (learning) what kind of approach in terms of timing and style is likely to work. As a result of this self-directed learning process, the content of the initiative is "owned" by the initiator; there is personal belief and conviction in it. Then, as the initiating proceeds, the leader reacts to (learns) the early effects of the initiative on others.

Furthermore, in developing an initiative through a process of self-directed learning, the managerial leader is also modeling (taking the lead) on a learning process that others in the organization need to follow if they are to come to understand, accept, and support the initiative. If the managerial leader is unconscious of the learning he or she has gone through, such modeling of a learning process for others can occur only very imperfectly, if at all. Indeed, forgetting what learning followers need to go through to understand and accept an initiative is a mistake leaders frequently make. In permanent white water, the managerial leader not only learns about what to do and proposes it to (or requires it of) others. He or she also leads others in learning what needs to be done, that is, takes the lead through leaderly learning.

We have to find more ways to help learners engage in self-directed leaderly learning. We have to stop simply telling them what they need to know, and find more ways to help them experience what they need to know and lead themselves in a learning process relevant to what they have discovered. Leaderly learners need to come to see that their ideas, passions, and initiatives will result from an ongoing learning process in their work. Leaders *discover* what acts of leadership are needed through a combination of their own self-directed efforts and their willingness to engage in the next of the qualities, creative learning.

Creative Leaderly Learning

In permanent white water, managerial leadership is usually exploration and discovery (see Resource II). Organizational members are constantly on what might be called process frontiers, where they must find ways of doing something they have never done before yet where there is little precedent or "best practice" to guide them (Vaill, 1989b). (The issues my successor deans were dealing with are all examples of process frontiers.)

A *process frontier* is a new area of activity for the organization or a substantial modification in the way something has been done heretofore. It is probably not a one-shot affair but a new and continuing area of activity. Process frontiers involve new attitudes, abilities, and actions. People are feeling their ways, even if they cannot quite admit it to themselves. Other organizations may be on similar process frontiers, which means cross-organizational learning is sometimes possible, provided someone takes the initiative (self-directed learning) to discover what others are doing. Process frontiers cannot be managed by already existing organizational policies, procedures, and traditions. Finally, process frontiers may continue to feel (feeling learning) like frontiers for an indefinite period of time, because in a world of permanent white water, we are not usually talking about simply replacing an old system with a new one.

One of the most difficult things about process frontiers is that goals are difficult to set with any confidence because so much is new. We have all had the experience of seeing some new process take twice as long to shake down as we had expected, or cost twice as much as we calculated, or bring with it a whole new set of problems we did not anticipate. The extreme goal directedness that institutional learning has built into our thinking does not always serve us well on process frontiers. Exploratory learning is not a matter of single-minded pursuit of a fixed objective.

It is in people's lives on process frontiers (for there may be several coexisting at any one time) that leaderly learning is occurring. The managerial leader-to-be needs to learn what that life is like, what kind of learning is needed on a process frontier, what kinds of help organizational members need in order to engage in that learning, and what his or her own role can best be to facilitate that learning. In most contemporary academic and corporate executive development programs, participants never hear about the learning that is needed on process frontiers, let alone what their own role in facilitating that learning might be. How learners can be helped to understand these things is itself a process frontier of major proportions for educators.

Institutional learning philosophy and practice have bred into many of us an obsession with "how to do it." This obsession amounts to a desire *not* to have a learning experience! We do not want to go through the creative learning that process frontiers require. Rather, we want a protocol that takes the messiness and the anxiety out of the process frontier. We want our learning to be targeted and efficient. But owing to the very nature of process frontiers and permanent white water, learning can be neither very targeted nor very efficient. The philosophy of learning as a way of being can do the learning process for leaderly learning no greater service than to expunge the idea that leaderly learning is primarily concerned with "how to do it."

Expressive Leaderly Learning

There is no element of learning as a way of being more central to managerial leadership than expressive learning. In Chapter One, I distinguished between the institutional learning approach—first learn, then express—and the approach inherent in learning as a way of being—learn in and through expression, learn from expression, learn by expressing. The traditional curricula in managerial leadership postpone or underplay expressiveness as a vehicle for learning. Expressiveness is seen as important but only as a testing ground for concepts already acquired through books and lectures. Expressiveness is seen as "application," as "practice," sometimes as literally a test of what has been learned in a passive conceptual mode.

In institutional learning, the primary interest in expressiveness is whether the intended conceptual understanding can be detected in the way the learner is expressing his or her learning. There is not much interest in the skill or artfulness of the expression itself. Stories abound of students who are marked down for getting the right answer but employing the wrong method or using the right method inappropriately. For example, a high school bandmaster sharply rebuked a drummer of my acquaintance for not looking at the sheet of music even though, as the drummer explained, he was not watching the music because he had memorized the score.

As I have remarked earlier, despite institutional learning's formal disinterest in expressive learning, it must also be said that throughout education and particularly in education for managerial leadership, we are living in a period of extraordinary ferment over expressive learning. Case studies are being made interactive so that the learner has to deal with the effects of his or her decisions. More emphasis is being placed on in-class exercises, on "living cases" where case characters join the class, on internships in ongoing organizations, on computer simulations and group projects, and on self-chosen and self-directed projects such as student-operated companies.

These innovations are very heartening, but there are a couple of major deficiencies in all this activity. First, the practice of institutional learning has already withstood an earlier major movement in "laboratory education"—an approach in which learners were encouraged to experiment with their behavior in the real time of the learning experience (Bradford and others, 1964)—and has managed to keep intact the philosophy of the relative unimportance of expressiveness. The physical arrangement of classrooms still reflects primarily institutional learning assumptions. The available space is filled with seats facing front (at my university, which I doubt is unique, this means as many seats as fire laws allow). Providing a way for learners to break up into groups or to engage in free-form expressive activity is a distant second priority in the use of space. Grades are still assigned, albeit quite awkwardly and sometimes apologetically.

Requisite instructor qualifications are still presumed to be determined by the content of the learning experience, not its process.

Second, the theory of the power of expressive learning remains underdeveloped, the province mainly of schools of education and so far not very evident in other academic fields, even though they may be experimenting with specific limited innovations. Without theoretical grounding, a learning project in expressiveness often rests only on the intuition of an individual instructor or facilitator and may be the first thing to go in a staffing crunch or a call for new content to be added to a curriculum.

Again, managerial leadership needs a worked-out theory of expressive learning as much or more than any other field. Managerial leadership *is* expressive, and it *is* learning. No matter what is done or not done in formal educational settings, the activity of managerial leadership itself remains expressive learning. The more learners can come to understand managerial leadership as expressive learning, the better prepared they are for the actual assumption of such roles.

There are three qualities of managerial leadership that combine to make it synonymous with expressive learning: (1) the individual's responsibility to impart purpose and direction to the system in which he or she is exercising managerial leadership; (2) the individual's inevitably partial knowledge of the nature of that system and its environment, within which purposes are pursued; and (3) the reactivity of the other human beings in the system to the initiatives of the managerial leader, meaning that the leader's actions must always take account not just of his or her own values and intentions but of the values and intentions of others as well. Take away any one or two of these qualities, and it might be possible to learn managerial leadership out of a book in a passive learning mode. The joint effects of all three, however, defy adequate abstract specification of what to do. In other words, there can be no cookbook. Managerial leadership can best be learned by attempting to *take* (express) decisions and actions that recognize the three qualities and their interrelations.

Meanwhile, until we have a worked-out theory of expressive learning, the least we can do is help learners understand that there can be no cookbook. We can stop asking them to memorize and regurgitate lists of managerial abilities. We can stop encouraging them to develop highly rationalized "courses of action" for "solving" a case study they are not a part of. We can work to help them understand that everything they do as managerial leaders will be from an attached, embedded position, where both their information and their latitude to act will be sharply limited by the realities of the situation. We can help them see how profoundly their effectiveness as managerial leaders depends on their *personal* expressiveness, not their ability to reproduce some generally appropriate "style" that "research" shows will "work" in a situation, as the misleading institutional learning image of what managerial leadership is all about encourages them to think.

Elsewhere, I have explored how the metaphor of management as a performing art helps us understand what is involved in the expressive quality of managerial leadership (Vaill, 1989a). In light of the previous discussion, I can suggest that performing artists have an additional experience that is highly instructive for learners of managerial leadership. They learn their art through performing it. They discover new depths in the soliloquy, the cadenza, the pas de deux, by performing it. Yes, by reflecting on it (reflexive learning); yes, by experimenting with it (creative learning); yes, by repeating it over and over (continual learning). But all these ways of learning presume that the performers are *doing* the activity in the first place—which is expressive learning. *Learners of managerial leadership have to try to lead*, and those facilitating their learning have to help them take this fateful step.

Feeling Leaderly Learning

During these last crowded days of the political crisis, my pulse had not quickened at any moment. I took it all as it came. But I cannot conceal from the reader of this

> truthful account that as I went to bed about 3 A.M., I was
> conscious of a profound sense of relief. At last I had the
> authority to give directions over the whole scene. I felt
> as if I were walking with Destiny, and that all my past life
> had been but a preparation for this hour and this trial
> [Churchill, 1948, p. 667].

Perhaps, given Winston Churchill's well-known instinct for self-dramatization, we should be careful not to attach too much significance to his famous account of his mood on becoming prime minister of Great Britain in May 1940. Still, even if we allow for a degree of exaggeration, his words make clear the role of feeling the meaning of one's learning. For it had been learning indeed that Churchill had been undergoing during the years of the buildup of the Nazi threat, and it would be learning that he would continue to do for the next five years. He had been trying desperately to impart the meanings that he felt to others throughout the 1930s. Now at last, as he says, he had authority to act on those learnings and meanings.

Similarly, Robert McNamara's account of his years as secretary of defense during the era of the Vietnam War can be read as a process of his gradually coming to feel the meaning of the events of the war, and particularly the meaning of the actions of the North Vietnamese, the Viet Cong, and the domestic antiwar protesters (McNamara, 1995). He is at pains to document how his thinking gradually changed from his energetic hawkishness of 1964 and 1965 to his advocacy in late 1967 of a policy that would lead to U.S. withdrawal (pp. 307–308). What is so clear in McNamara's account is the powerful meaning to him of the war data streaming into his office from all over the world. These were not dry facts and trends; their human meaning contained powerful learning for him. He let himself feel his meanings change as the data changed, although as he makes clear, it was often very painful to feel the meaning of this data because it put him increasingly into opposition with the military hierarchy as well as with many knowledgeable civilians inside and outside the Johnson administration. At one point, he notes that from a distance of thirty years, he can now see that facts in hand were pointing toward winding down the war at least six months earlier than he consciously reached that conclusion in November 1967 (p. 271).

Both Churchill and McNamara make very clear that a leaderly learner is not calmly keeping score on the surrounding world, noting which events are advantageous and which disadvantageous. Facts do not speak for themselves, for if they did, humans would find it easy to agree. Meanings, implications, significances, and portents are *wrested* from the flow of events, wrested by men and women who have a felt stake in how things are unfolding.

Furthermore, felt meanings themselves can be frequently equivocal. There can be conflicts between the interests of various parties to a situation, between personal values and what is good for the institution, between desire for immediate success and long-term viability, between looking good and *being* good. This is the province of "the loneliness of command."

But the fact that feelings can be mercurial and contradictory does not mean they should be banished from the leaderly learner's awareness. We do not do beginning leaderly learners a service by letting them think that managerial leaders solve problems rationally and that their feeling for situations plays little part. As Barnard says, a managerial leader engages in "sensing the organization as a whole and the total situation relevant to it. [This sensing] transcends the capacity of merely intellectual methods. . . . The terms pertinent to it are 'feeling,' 'judgment,' 'sense,' 'proportion,' 'balance,' 'appropriateness.' It is a matter of art rather than science, and is aesthetic rather than logical" (1938, p. 235).

Without such qualities as Barnard mentions, leaderly learning is mechanical. It is drudgery. It does not excite the person engaging in it, and it certainly is unlikely to impress the subordinates who will be affected by the managerial leader's learning and be expected to participate in it. Environmental scanning should be driven by *curiosity*; it is not just an obligatory step in a strategic planning model. Employee empowerment is a *gift* given in a spirit of support, in addition to being good behavioral science. Competitiveness is a *feeling*, supposedly an indispensable one for successful managerial leaders. Concern for the customer is a *feeling*. It is probably not an exaggeration to say that every action a managerial leader might take has its feeling component. Learning the action entails developing the accompanying feeling. Thus, feeling leaderly learning is not just a luxury or some piece of New-Age romanticism. It is central to whether leaderly learning occurs at all.

On-Line Leaderly Learning

There should be no debate about the value of on-the-job-training and thus of on-the-job leaderly learning in particular. Expressive learning counsels that a person prepares for leaderly learning by beginning right away to explore what can be learned as he or she tries to do the things managerial leaders do. On-line leaderly learning counsels that the beginning leaderly learner needs to practice expressiveness in genuine operating situations, not just through exercises, simulations, and other surrogates. In the real world, the quality of one's leaderly learning *matters* to oneself and others inside and outside the organization. This is the indispensable experience— the realization that one's learning is going to matter in terms of actual consequences. It is one thing to practice writing dismissal letters in a business communications workshop and quite another to write and sign a document that could result in a lawsuit. The longer the real-world significance of a person's learning is postponed, the less prepared he or she is to engage in productive on-line leaderly learning when the time finally does come to act within an organization. Institutional learning practices might be seen as a kind of learning drug and on-line leaderly learning as drug detoxification. The beginner needs to find out something about this quality of learning as a way of being.

The logistics of helping learners engage in on-line learning are difficult, to be sure. Too often for too many years, however, management educators have let logistical barriers be decisive. Most management programs in higher education still take place predominantly in classrooms. What if we reversed the priorities? What if we said the primary responsibility of academics is to make sure the learner understands the on-line environment and the kind of learning that is possible there? In formal classes and workshops then, we could help learners interpret and synthesize past on-line learnings and plan new ones, and also reflect on how on-line environments differ in their learning potential from the formal classroom. This would be a very different philosophy of leaderly learning than the one that presently reigns supreme. But it is the inability of the present institutional learning model to foster leaderly learning that makes consideration of more radical approaches urgent.

Continual Leaderly Learning

How do learners understand the idea of lifelong learning—assuming that they accept the notion that education does not end with the cessation of formal schooling? This question would make a fascinating research project. My belief, based on conversations with learners in management programs over many years, is that we can hypothesize at least two general answers to the question. First, learners' image of lifelong learning tends to be one simply of constant accumulation of new information—what Karl Popper called a "bucket theory of the mind" (Miller, 1985, pp. 105–106); they equate lifelong learning with uncritically piling new information on top of old information for the rest of their careers. Second, they do not have a well-formed image of what the learning process will be like on the practical level. They know that it will be somewhat different from formal educational systems, but they do not know exactly how. While they may not like institutional learning philosophy and practice very much, they have not mentally crystallized an alternative set of learning processes. Taken together, these two hypotheses say that most learners have not thought much at all about what lifelong learning really means.

Learners need to grasp more fully what lifelong learning is. If they do not, the understanding that managerial leadership is learning (the guiding proposition of this chapter) will be lost on them. As managerial leaders, they will be forced into lifelong learning because that goes with the territory, but they will be unprepared to take charge of their learning through self-directed learning; they will not be comfortable taking risks with their learning and thus will lack creative learning; they will not understand why learning expressively and on-line are the most effective methods open to them; and they will not be freed of the burdensome feelings about learning in which their institutional learning has trained them, thus they will lack feeling learning. Continual leaderly learning is necessary because ongoing change demands it. Learning as a way of being understood as life process is the key, I believe, to personal effectiveness and mental health in permanent white water. Conversely, when misunderstood as just one more set of onerous responsibilities, lifelong learning becomes an overwhelming and possibly terrifying burden.

Reflexive Leaderly Learning

In Chapter Two, I hypothesized characteristics of a reflective beginner at some length. However, one point not made there is that beginning itself is a potentially reflexive process, provided a learner has a way of thinking that makes this process possible. Can we let beginnings reflexively teach us about beginning? Years of exposure to institutional learning have filled us with self-consciousness, self-doubt, and shame about being beginners—not a very good frame of mind for learning about being a beginner and how to begin well. If being a beginner is potentially reflexive, then leaderly learning is also potentially reflexive: leaderly learning potentially teaches us about leaderly learning—that is what reflexive learning is all about.

How might a leaderly learner experience improvement in his or her learning processes? In general, the answer is the same one I gave in Chapter Two—through improvement in his or her practice of the first six qualities of learning as a way of being. As each of those six qualities singly and in combination provides specific learning experiences, the managerial leader can simultaneously observe whether he or she is learning more fully, more comfortably, and/or more effectively than on a previous occasion. In the unending cycle of observation and improvement is the reflexivity. More specifically, it is through such reflection that a leaderly learner will discover the learning challenges built into specific subject matters—provided he or she is paying attention to their emergence. Reflexivity is a potential quality of learning not an automatic one. It is very easy to have the same experience over and over without learning anything about the nature of the learning challenge it poses.

Reflexivity also illuminates another dimension of leaderly learning not mentioned thus far. Managerial leaders cannot learn everything. They have to pick and choose the topics they will focus on learning and the topics they will let go. My observation of my successor deans has made it clear to me that each action an executive takes leads on to certain new learning experiences and forecloses others. Managerial leaders literally choose, in real time, the kinds of learning experiences and learning challenges they are going to have. The question is not whether this happens, but whether managerial leaders are going to be consciously reflective about it. Where should their learning energy go? On which process frontiers is it especially important for the boss to be having a rich learning experience?

Three Leaderly Learning Choices: Technical, Purposeful, and Relational

At the beginning of this chapter, I noted the enormous amount of material available on the subject of what managerial leaders do and how they ought to act. We could ask of any one of these formulations, what is the *process* by which a learner is to learn all of these sterling qualities and abilities?[1]

Out of all the things that have been and are being said about the attitudes and abilities of the effective managerial leader, the following three broad areas of necessary knowledge and skill seem to arise repeatedly: technical, purposeful, and relational. The managerial leader with technical knowledge and skill is continually learning, in some depth, the technical facts of the organization's activities; he or she is constantly doing the necessary homework in order to articulate purposes and work with others from a base of valid knowledge. A leader with purposeful knowledge and skill (Vaill, 1982) is immersed in a continual process of establishing broad directions and specific goals and building clarity, consensus, and commitment regarding what the organization is going to do. Purposing includes establishing a "mission" and a "vision"—two leadership activities highly endorsed in current management literature and education. A leader with relational knowledge and skill makes purposes and technical facts and realities meaningful to all the various stakeholders he or she encounters. This ability includes one-on-one sensitivity, proficiency in working in teams, and one-to-many effectiveness, and it especially includes conducting oneself in an honest and psychologically and spiritually healthy manner.

Obviously the technical, the purposeful, and the relational abilities are interrelated; or to put it the other way around, in areas where they are not interrelated, the individual probably does not exhibit effective managerial leadership. Technical skill that is empty of purposeful or relational ability, or both, can be merely fussing with details, "bean counting," as we say. Purposing that fails to be grounded in an accurate understanding of the facts can be indifferent to the delicate process of making itself meaningful to others.

1.   Four books that do focus specifically on *how* people can develop themselves as managerial leaders are Cantor (1958); McCall, Lombardo, and Morrison (1988); Bennis and Nanus (1985); and Clark and Clark (1994).

Relating that is weak on technical matters and/or purpose can devolve into politicking and obsequiousness.

Even though these three abilities are obviously interrelated, formal educational environments tend to teach them in an uninterrelated fashion. And a further word needs to be said about technical ability especially. Institutional learning tends to focus on developing this ability in terms of the learner's capacity to deal with all the various facts and methodologies that are relevant to what an organization does. This includes the study of economic and financial factors, of legal matters, of the operational realities of an organization's various mechanical and electronic systems, and of the intricacies of management systems for planning and controlling activity. Over the last forty years, this enormous body of technical material has come to be equated with what a professional degree in management is all about. The hard work of going to business school is the assimilating (in institutional learning terms) of this large and constantly growing mass of material. In popular mythology, what an M.B.A. graduate is "good at" is skillfully devouring data with all these technical methods, on behalf of stockholders and other stakeholders. The technical dimension is what has caused managerial education to become virtually synonymous with number crunching.

It is increasingly clear, however, that equating managerial leadership with possessing an enormous amount of technical knowledge has been a strategic mistake. There is just too much evidence that technical knowledge by itself does not result in leadership. The purposeful and relational abilities are indispensable if an individual's technical knowledge and skill and ability to learn further technical material are to pay off for an organization in the way the organization intends.

If we focused on the learning challenges of technical knowledge and skill, we would discover that the subject's intrinsic complexity and density is not the main challenge. Instead, the main learning challenge of the technical is to *keep it linked to the purposeful and the relational*. We understand this about the other two abilities:

purposing has to have content (the technical) and it has to be meaningful to others (the relational). Relating has to have direction (purpose) and it, too, has to have content (the technical)—we need something to relate to each other *about*. But in our technique-ridden culture, we become preoccupied with soaking up facts and techniques, and we forget that the technical is only meaningful in terms of the purposes to which it is put and the human meanings and relationships that it enriches. Perhaps there is no greater challenge for lifelong leaderly learning than ongoing learning of the *interrelationships* of the technical, the purposeful, and the relational.

Conclusion

This has been a chapter that is not about leadership per se—but about learning leadership, or as I have suggested we call it, leaderly learning. Our argument has been that the learning challenges of effective leadership have not been sufficiently studied. We have not incorporated ideas about learning as a way of being into our thinking about how leading is learned. Behind these notions is a more basic one—that managerial leadership itself is primarily learning. There is nothing static about it, nothing fixed, nothing constant from person to person or from situation to situation. Instead, it is a moment-to-moment process of grasping (learning) the needs and opportunities for influence that are found in situations and realizing (learning) what purposeful things one can do there.

Perhaps just as a coda we might take note of the passive, academic mood this word "leadership" puts us into. How ironic that such a dynamic and energetic form of human activity—leading—should be discussed among serious people with a suffix that means a fixed, static quality!

* * * * * * *

Of all the new and different things managerial leaders are doing, poised on their organizational process frontiers, one of the most challenging is establishing cross-cultural relationships. Cross-cultural understanding will be a prime determinant of a leader's effectiveness for the foreseeable future. The next chapter discusses why cultural learning as a way of being must be as much about *un*learning the old as it is about positively learning the new.

5

· ·

Cultural Unlearning

Consider the following twelve vignettes of situations in which any of us might find ourselves. It is experiences like these that are convincing managerial leaders that it is important to learn about culture and about cross-cultural relationships.

1. You are landing in the main international airport of a country that you have never been to before and are due at the hotel where you are to stay to begin meeting with those in this country you have come to see.

2. A person of your sex and approximate age and status, but from another culture, is speaking to you about a matter of significance to you both. Yet you can hardly understand the person even though he or she is speaking your language.

3. You are dressing for a very important occasion in another culture where both business and social activities will be combined. There will be people in attendance who are interested in meeting you.

4. You find yourself becoming increasingly ill a couple of hours after attending a large banquet in another culture. You are in your room in the hotel. You are unfamiliar with the customs or language of this culture. It is 1:30 A.M.

5. You have just finished a presentation to the president of a company in another culture, proposing a relationship between his company and yours. He now begins to speak in his language so rapidly that the interpreter can hardly keep up. All the outward signs of his behavior and attitude are consistent with what in your culture would mean extreme anger.

6. You are heading home after an enjoyable and successful two-month stay in another country where you have negotiated several business deals that you know will be very pleasing to your associates back home.

7. On very short notice, you are traveling to a culture known for its strange and exotic ways. You have never had any contact with it before. Just before leaving, you collected a large number of maps, brochures, travel handbooks, and commercial information on this culture. The reason for your trip is to investigate the causes of shortages in critical supplies that your organization imports from this culture.

8. Important foreign visitors are coming to your company, and you have been put in charge of all the arrangements for their housing, entertainment, and travel while they are in your city.

9. Your company has a subsidiary in another culture that has become quite controversial. You have newspaper articles collected of what is being said about the subsidiary and had them translated into your language. On reading the translations, you find them full of incorrect information and emotional attacks on both the subsidiary and the parent company that you work for in your own country.

10. You go to work for a company outside your country, in a culture where family relationships are very important. You, of course, have no family ties in the company. As time goes on, you find that virtually all significant communications and all

promotions and distributions of other rewards seem to you to be linked to whose family one is in or to some other close personal tie one has to higher-level managers.

11. You fall in love with a person from a culture that you know is extremely poorly thought of in your home culture.

12. When you return after an extended stay abroad in several different cultures, your friends back home tell you that you have changed a lot. They imply that they do not like you as much as they did before you left on your cross-cultural adventures.

These situations could happen to anyone—and regularly do. Our commonsense assumption is that in each case, if we knew enough about the other culture involved, we would be able to act effectively and solve whatever problem the situation contains. This is a direct result of the institutional learning philosophy that we have absorbed. It is that philosophy that tells us the key to these situations is to learn more about the cultures in question before such situations arise. We would do this learning through off-line study and through direct exposure.

This approach is not necessarily wrong. It has produced a rapidly growing cottage industry of giving advice about different cultures, often in the form of books such as Axtell's *Do's and Taboos around the World* (1993), and I certainly do not condemn off-line study of other cultures or discourage learners from having as much direct contact with other cultures as possible. However, I believe that there is also a different approach, one intended for a present and future world containing two conditions that the philosophy and practice of institutional learning have not anticipated. First, the sheer amount of cross-cultural contact is exploding for all cultures and for all levels of society and walks of life in each culture. In assuming that situations like the twelve just sketched can be dealt with simply by learning more and more about other cultures, the practice of institutional learning ignores that such challenges and puzzles are potentially infinite in number and that there are thousands of cultures and subcultures available to produce them. In other words, it is an error to think one can *prepare* adequately for such situations—the variety of ways in which they can arise is too vast.

The second evolving condition is that more and more we play action-taking roles in the world of work, roles that require problem-solving conversations with members of other cultures, leadership of them and from them, and close interpersonal relationships. In other words, the actions we take to solve and resolve situations like those in the vignettes will have future consequences for our relationships with the others involved. Our credibility and effectiveness ride on how we act, and large amounts of money and other resources can be at stake. Tourists and other short-term visitors to other cultures do not usually have to live with the results of their cross-cultural actions. The tourist can laughingly recall "getting Montezuma's revenge and missing the trip to the Mayan ruins." The executive does not laugh in recalling how an inability to access the right health services resulted in a lost contract and embarrassment for his or her company.

These situations, furthermore, do not arise only for someone traveling to another national culture. The challenges described can also arise in any subculture of a national culture (Cross, 1994). The United States, Great Britain, South Africa, India, China, Brazil, and Russia are just a few examples of richly multicultural societies in which even national citizenship is no guarantee that one will understand and be able to adapt to all the cultural differences that are present. Owing to the present global patterns of migration, virtually all countries of the developed world are becoming thoroughly multicultural. Situations are proliferating in which the standards of two or more cultures are involved in determining the correctness of a course of action. National boundaries are no longer deciding factors in determining what is cross-cultural.

Learning as a Way of Being as an Alternative Approach

An alternative strategy for coping with situations like those I have described is to discover *in the real time of the situation* how to act effectively. When we can do this, we become less dependent on prior experience or prior study for guidance in the particular situation. Learning our way through situations like the ones mentioned is the process of learning as a way of being. We do not learn first, and then "handle" these situations. Rather, in the handling *is* the learning as a way of being. In other words, along the lines discussed in Chapter Two, we can ask what might it mean to learn to be a "reflective *cultural* beginner"? This is not an approach that institutional learning-dominated cultural education has considered. That education teaches us to be deathly afraid of cross-cultural faux pas and assumes that the way to prevent them is to be thoroughly prepared for any situation we might get into. But again, this is an unrealistic expectation.

The vignettes that open this chapter are deliberately phrased from the reader's point of view. I encourage you to put yourself into these situations and imagine the thoughts and feelings you might be having if you were actually experiencing each situation. Not all situations will stir all readers, of course. For any given situation, you might well respond, "So what's the problem?" Which is to say, "I think if I were in this situation, I would know what to do. I would not be confused or angry or afraid." But I hope every reader will be able to find a few vignettes (or to think of analogous situations) where a little knot of confusion or anger or fear does flicker and tighten inside. You remember. The time when——.

That little knot is about not knowing how to act, and not knowing how to act is the essence of the challenge of cross-cultural situations. The institutional learning model tells us to seek a formula, as I have said. But there are not enough formulas, and they are not precise enough to fit the unique texture of a live situation, and they quickly get out of date in the rapidly evolving cultural relationships of the modern world. What is needed instead is a learner with the ability and the willingness to risk, to experiment, to learn from feedback, and above all to enjoy the adventure of *discovering* how to act when the rules of the learner's home culture are clearly off and the learner is out in the open between cultures.

This notion of being between cultures is important. "When in Rome . . ." is always inadequate advice because, in the final analysis, those of us who are not from Rome cannot duplicate Romans. We can emulate Romans, ape Romans, take detailed notes on Romans and commit the notes to memory, but we cannot become Romans—not in any reasonable period of time, at least. We can never be more than non-Romans-trying-to-act-enough-like-Romans-so-that-no-one-will-notice. This condition is quite interesting from a learning point of view, indeed, from an identity point of view. Since we non-Romans cannot truly become Romans, there is the possibility that in copying the Romans, we might get a behavior or an attitude wrong *from the outset*. As pioneering anthropologist Edward Sapir wrote:

> It is impossible to say what an individual is doing unless we have accepted the essentially arbitrary modes of interpretation that social tradition is constantly suggesting to us from the very moment of our birth. Let anyone who doubts this try the experiment of making a painstaking report . . . of the actions of a group of natives engaged in some activity, say religious, to which he has not the cultural key. . . . If he is a skillful writer, he may succeed in giving a picturesque account of what he sees and hears, but the chances of his being able to give a relation of what happens, in terms that would be acceptable and intelligible to the natives themselves, are practically nil. He will be guilty of all manner of distortion; his emphasis will be constantly askew. He will find interesting what the natives take for granted as a casual kind

of behavior worthy of no particular comment, and he will utterly fail to observe the crucial turning points in the course of action that give formal significance to the whole in the minds of those who do possess the key to its understanding [quoted in Harris, 1968, pp. 570–571].

Presumably, learning as a way of being would help a learner avoid the problem Sapir depicts. Sapir's observer is clearly in the institutional learning mode of trying to write down the factual nature of an alien situation. As Sapir notes, however, the observer cannot take a verbal photograph of a situation to which "he has not the cultural key." That cultural key will come only from the varieties of learning as a way of being, because it is inside the situation, inside the participants' meanings. Contrary to what institutional learning assumes, *participatory* cultural knowledge—that is, knowledge that qualifies us to participate in a given event—cannot be acquired by remaining outside the situation and treating it like an academic subject. All twelve of the cross-cultural situations I have described require participatory cultural knowledge. The person in the situation has to do something, something *in relation to* other actors in the situation, whose actions will then in turn influence what the focal person does next. (This is what Karl Weick, 1979, called a "double interact," arguing that such interacts were the fundamental units of analysis in understanding social behavior.) Learning as a way of being is a process of acquiring participatory cultural knowledge in the real time of situations, using the seven interrelated qualities of that learning to discover a cultural key for the situation at hand.

Two Dimensions of Cultural Keys

Cultural key is a metaphorical not an exact phrase. A cultural key is an understanding of the meaning of a given situation from the point of view of those cultural representatives who are involved in it in any way, both those of the culture in which the situation is occurring and those of other cultures. In addition, because the meaning of any situation is essentially unbounded, no one cultural key can be, or needs to be, a complete understanding of that meaning. For example, ceremonies marking the fiftieth anniversary of the end of World War II are being conducted as this book goes to press. Consider the many different layers of meaning such ceremonies have—for past participants and their families, for military currently on active duty, for political leaders, for the media that report the ceremonies, for historians, and for the young whose grasp of the events commemorated is minimal. A cultural key to such situations is both finite and infinite—finite in the sense that through learning as a way of being one could achieve a reasonable understanding even on partial information, but infinite in the sense that there is really no limit to learning the depth or intensity or significance of such events.

A cultural key to the meaning of a situation, then, is not a fact about the situation but a *perception* by a participant or an observer. Any perception involves both a perceived and a perceiver. A cultural key thus resides both in the details of the situation and in the perceptual ability of an observer or member. A cultural key is not self-knowledge, and it is not other-knowledge. It is knowledge of self-in-relation-to-other.[1] This means there is no *one* effective course of action for each of the sample situations sketched previously; there is a whole family of effective courses of action, depending on the culture of the person who has the problem in relation to the culture in which the problem is occurring. Once again, our institutional learning habits betray us when they lead us to assume there will be one best answer to each situation.

For there to be one best answer, the culture of either the perceived or the perceiver would have to be suppressed. Indeed, what

1.   Technically, all knowledge has this relational quality. Meaning lies between us as perceivers and what we perceive. However, there are few other subjects—esthetics would be one—where the relational quality of knowledge is as clear as it is in cross-cultural learning.

we call ethnocentricity is the very common habit of suppressing the "data pole," that is, the details of the situation, in favor of the perceiver's categories and values. It is our unconscious and very deep-seated tendency to look at the world through our own spectacles that has led me to use the term *unlearning* rather than *learning* in the title of this chapter. Finding a cultural key to unfamiliar situations is *unlearning as a way of being!*

How, then, do we unlearn? We cannot literally erase the existing neural connections in our brains. Therefore, I am not counseling that we press "delete" but rather "reveal codes."[2] As Sapir notes, learning a cultural key involves "accepting the essentially arbitrary modes of interpretation [of] social tradition." His realization is extremely important. Our own arbitrary modes make sense to us. Another culture's arbitrary modes may look mysterious or irrational. We can see the arbitrariness in someone else's diet or habits or ways of thinking; it is harder to see it in our own. The question is, how do we go about accepting some other culture's arbitrary modes as having the same kind of validity as our own? The answer is that to accept another culture's modes, we do not have to approve of them, but we do have to acknowledge that their reality is coequal with the modes of our own culture. If we admit the coequality of the other culture's modes, it means we regard the human beings who adhere to those other modes as just as important as the human beings in our own culture. This difference between acceptance on the one hand and approval on the other is one of the most elusive distinctions in cross-cultural understanding. Over and over, even when we think we appreciate the distinction, we find ourselves slipping back into an evaluative stance, picking and choosing what about another culture we like and what we do not like, using our own culture as a benchmark.

Acceptance, then, requires a kind of unlearning, a look at codes, a granting that there are realities and meanings that may be quite

2. There may be a few readers on whom this distinction is lost. "Reveal codes" is a command in word processing software that displays on the screen all the embedded commands that control the format of a document, such as paragraphing, type styles, underlining, and the like. The "delete" command, of course, erases material.

different from those taught by our own culture. The process of unlearning involves becoming more aware (by using reflexive learning) of two operations that we normally perform unconsciously.

Relativity of Perception

First, we must become more aware of the operation of our own perceptual tendencies, including the assumptions we make, the values we apply, and the positive and negative feelings we experience when situations confirm or challenge our assumptions and values (Athos and Gabarro, 1978, chap. 5). Cultures condition their members in a unique common psychology (see Vaill, 1989a, chap. 10). The regular production over time of numbers of individuals with the same unique common psychology is what qualifies a human system to be called a culture, as opposed to merely a social grouping or to a work organization that employs selected attributes of people. Social groupings and work organizations can be cultures, of course; they are just not such automatically. Members of a true culture have been *shaped*. However, their shaping occurs extremely subtly, over a substantial period of time, and in the case of children, completely out of their awareness. The unique common psychology of the culture comes to permeate each member's being, becomes the natural and often the only way that the person knows for making sense of his or her experience. Unlearning, then, is a developing awareness in each of us of how our unique common psychology has been developed by the dominant culture of our lives.

Keen (1975, pp. 37–40) has provided a framework that is simple and practical for understanding our unconscious perceptual tendencies and thus for the process of real-time discovery of our unique common psychology in cross-cultural situations. ("Unconscious," of course, is not used in the Freudian sense to mean that these tendencies are repressed due to their anxiety-producing character, only that they are out of conscious awareness and taken for granted.) Keen draws on the phenomenological tradition (Husserl, 1970; Zaner, 1970) for the purposes of understanding oneself and others more deeply and validly. While he does not explicitly apply his framework to cross-cultural situations, considering it more generic than that, it seems particularly useful when we are feeling the confusion, anger, and fear that often accompany cross-cultural experience. The three sequential elements of his approach are the "phenomenological reduction," the "imaginative variation," and the "interpretation."

A *phenomenological reduction* is a decision to try to let the thing we encounter be what it is, separate from our perception of it. This entails a recognition of our natural tendency to impute meaning to it, to have already decided what it means. Instead, we are to back up from the meaning we naturally assign and try to open ourselves to the thing or situation as it is. For example, a phenomenological reduction on the eighth situation described earlier, in which we are in charge of arrangements for foreign visitors to our company, might involve seeing the visit for what it is rather than augmented and perhaps distorted by its personal significance to us. Visits qua visits— what are they? Well, they are full of unfamiliarity. There are always glitches. They have a one-of-a-kind quality and are difficult to program or control exactly. Inevitably, individual foibles of both visitors and visited intrude on plans. Visitors themselves understand some of these things and are in a different frame of mind than when at home. People "make allowances" on visits. Visits are also unpredictable in their consequences because there is no way of guaranteeing what kind of a time the visitors will have. In general, visits are full of emergences as well as emergencies. These are some thoughts that might come to mind as we let the *being* of visits *be*, but by no means are these ideas exhaustive. (The reader is encouraged to perform his or her own reduction on this or another cross-cultural situation.)

As we let the reality of the being of the phenomenon emerge, it becomes possible for us to perform the second of the three operations Keen describes—imaginative variation. *Imaginative variation* is the almost playful combining and recombining of the various modes of the situation's being. What is called brainstorming, for example, is actually a form of imaginative variation. Continuing with the example of the foreign visitors, as we reflected on the visit as such, we would become aware of the variety of conditions affecting the visit: its purpose, the agenda, the time available, the resources of the visitors, the importance to the hosts of the visit, activities of the hosts that are unconnected to the visit, the weather, and so on. It would become clear that there are an infinity of potential visits embedded in the situation, depending on how all these variables play out. As the variables and their possible states became conscious, we could begin combining them into various scenarios, noting which variables we would need to be able to control to produce which scenario and noting which variables we would not be able to control. The act of imaginative variation actively releases the phenomenon from the control of our values and perceptual categories. We begin to see what a *profusion* any situation actually is.

Out of this process, we could begin to form *interpretations* of the likelihood and the desirability of the various scenarios. With this third step, we begin to settle on what the visit is likely to mean and what its significance is for ourselves. Unlike the intuitive and relatively unconscious interpretation we might have arrived at, this three-stage framework has the advantage of being conscious and reflective, so that as the variables do begin to play out on the visit, there are fewer surprises and hence less chance of our experiencing confusion, anger, and fear in the cross-cultural interaction.

Keen's framework constitutes learning as a way of being. The seven qualities of that learning are all at play as the phenomenological reduction is performed and imaginative variations and interpretations are made. The entire three-phase process is energized by self-directed learning, without which it would not be possible. The reduction is a particularly interesting kind of creative and expressive learning. We are not just thinking *about* the phenomenon when we engage in creative and expressive learning; instead, we are undertaking an active exploration of its being. Feeling learning occurs vividly as imaginative variations are made. In fact, because imaginative variations are not merely abstract permutations of the phenomenon, they are probably not possible without feeling learning. Interpretation requires reflexive learning in particular, letting the reduction and the imaginative variations teach us about the meaning and significance of the phenomenon. All twelve of the sample situations above are cases of on-line learning. They are not artificial exercises but real situations in which one might find oneself. Finally, the framework should be gone through repeatedly as a situation unfolds; the mentality of continual learning is necessary. The key point in Keen's framework is the thinking through of an experience. This thinking through is not done merely in anticipation of the event. It is done on-line throughout the event. As the event unfolds, we can perform new reductions on it continually, as well as new imaginative variations and new interpretations.

Clearly, then, learning as a way of being weaves all through the three steps we might take in order to transcend the confusion, anger, and fear that can arise when our actions are contingent on cultural standards that are not our own.

Meaning Is Context

I have been describing an approach to cross-cultural situations that involves a rather intense effort to both expand and enrich our natural perceptual tendencies. The aim is to discover possible meanings that may not automatically spring to mind, indeed, meanings that may be blocked from our minds under normal circumstances by the culturally conditioned assumptions and values that we carry with us. Another culture's traditional meanings may be literally unimaginable to us without the particular kind of effort advocated here.

When we use Keen's generic process in a cross-cultural situation, it describes what we should try to do with our awareness of that situation in order to understand it more deeply and attain a cultural key to it. But by itself, the process permits us to deconstruct a situation in virtually any way that we please. Since the assumption is that a cross-cultural learner will be doing much of this work in the real time of an unfolding situation, more focus than this process provides is needed.

Edward Hall makes a powerful case for the idea that the thing to understand about any action is the *context* in which it is occurring; that actions and events do not have meaning independently of context; and that context is an invisible system of "givens" for members of a culture, a system that creates and sustains the intelligibility of all their actions. What is needed is an effective way of thinking about context, which can then be applied using the seven qualities of learning as a way of being. The point here is not that we first use Keen's framework and then Hall's ideas about context, or the reverse. Rather, we try to practice the framework while focusing on the context within which the cross-cultural event or problem we do not understand is occurring. We focus phenomenological reduction on context. We engage in imaginative variation of context. We interpret how meaning for a culture's members depends on context.

As an example, take flag burning. For one thing, the meaning depends heavily on who is perceiving the flag burning. But beyond that, the meaning of flag burning is one thing if it is performed on Veterans' Day by a group of obviously nonmilitary youths and interrupts a commemorative ceremony on the steps of the U.S. Capitol. The meaning is quite another thing if we add to this context klieg lights, sound booms, costume and prop people, police lines to keep back the gawkers, and an imperious director striding back and forth shouting commands. Hardly anyone would be moved to mayhem by the latter context; many Americans (note how a scenario of behavior may easily be able to take nationality for granted) might be moved to physical violence in the former context. (To extend the significance of nationality, note that even the first context would not move many Americans to mayhem if it was the flag of another nation that was being burned—another example of how small details of context can have large consequences for meaning.)

Context is also affected by action. If a fist fight is acceptable within a particular context, for example, and is supported by such contextual factors as time and place and the reasons the parties have for fighting, the whole context can nevertheless shift instantly if one person pulls out a knife or a gun. A killing weapon becomes a new contextual element that changes the meaning of the whole event. Context and actions-within-context stand in an interdependent relationship.

When the context is our home culture, we have learned how to perceive it instantaneously and to then know what kinds and degrees of behavior are and are not appropriate. When we see everyday situations within a culture—a normal street scene, for example—we are seeing people behaving within the boundaries of what is appropriate in that culture. If we see some members pushing the limits—disrobing, for example—then we see quickly activated new contextual forces, some subtly reproving and some brutally repressive, for restoring "sanity" to the context.

Hall's unique contribution (1977) in this area has been to suggest a scheme for understanding the context of any situation. He offers five categories of data that are present in any situation and that taken as a system of interacting factors, establish a context, or frame, that provides the grounds of meaning for the actions that occur. The difficulty we typically have with context is that it is normally invisible. Our cultures teach us to keep it invisible, not deliberately but because contextual factors are taught to us as unremarkable and taken-for-granted facts. We have to unlearn a context's invisibility by thinking about it, by reflecting on what in a situation makes some kinds of behavior quite appropriate and other kinds quite inappropriate. Hall's scheme and the embellishments it invites help us begin to do this.

The five categories of contextual factors that Hall proposes are (1) the *subject* or *activity* that is the event itself, (2) the kind of *situation* the event is occurring in, (3) the *roles and statuses* of those involved, (4) individuals' *past experiences* with situations containing these same contextual factors, and (5) the *way the situation is defined* by the broader culture within which it is occurring (1977, pp. 87–90). A wedding, for example, is a particular kind of event in a particular situation (factors 1 and 2), in which it makes a difference who the parties are (factor 3), the kind and amount of past experience the various parties have with weddings like this one (factor 4), and what the broader culture says about this kind of wedding attended by these kinds of people (factor 5). In the case of a wedding, all these contexts occur within a larger context that describes behavior. Weddings vary widely depending on other contextual factors, but no one would expect the groomsmen to start playing frisbee in the hall as the ceremony was occurring. (Although such jumping radically out of context is the secret of much of the best comedy, as performers like the Monty Python troupe, Mel Brooks, and David Letterman demonstrate repeatedly.) The context that the five factors describe profoundly affects the meaning of such events as either the bride or groom not showing up, or the best man forgetting the ring, or the bride's and groom's fathers getting into a heated argument; or the caterer providing tainted food. The *meaning* of any of these events changes as the wedding context changes.

Hall's categories are useful, but even more, they are stimulating. Contextual analysis, especially as might be performed on the fly by involved participants, is an idea in its infancy. It pays to consider other contextual categories than the five already mentioned. Time of day or of the week, month, or year, for example, can be a powerful contextual factor. We do things on holidays that we do not do on work days and vice versa. We do things in the summer that we do not do in the winter and vice versa. We might not "see" someone swimming on a Saturday afternoon in July in the Northern Hemisphere because that action would be wholly "in context." The same person at the same time of day doing the same thing in mid-January would probably catch our eye. Another category of context might be the number of people present in the situation. Things that are appropriate in small groups are inappropriate in large groups and vice versa.

In general, I suggest that we think of Hall and other contextual theorists as pointing in a fruitful direction, but that we also employ our self-directed, creative, expressive, and reflective learning to improve our understanding of the structure of contexts. The combination of creative and expressive learning might be particularly useful here: the creative part would be to think up things we might do in various contexts to see how they "play"; the expressive part would be to do them and learn about context from what happens. Employees do this with new supervisors all the time, engaging in "testing" behaviors of one kind or another to see how the boss will react. It is as if they were asking experimentally, "What kind of authority is going to be part of the context with this new boss?" (More broadly, the kind of authority present in any situation might be another contextual category to consider adding to Hall's scheme.)

I am suggesting that in learning as a way of being, we as cultural unlearners focus on contexts that are familiar, that we learn to look anew at things formerly taken for granted. Then, as the use of a framework becomes more habitual, it will be appropriate for us to move into increasingly unfamiliar contexts. The general question we ask as unlearners is, Why does this behavior I am looking at make sense in this context? To ask the question *is* the unlearning, because within our own familiar contexts, our culture has already taught us the answer.

Some Examples of Unlearning Methods

Over the years, I have had occasion to invent various methods for helping unlearners come to think about some of the matters just discussed. This chapter closes with a listing and brief description of ten of these methods. They are examples of my own creative and expressive learning as I work on-line in my environments of classrooms, workshops, and consulting. My aim is to encourage the reader in his or her own creative and expressive learning on these subjects, as well as to share some of my own discoveries.

1. *Twelve situations.* The twelve vignettes that open this chapter were created originally as discussion vehicles for multicultural groupings. Discussion participants typically have an extraordinary unlearning experience as the multiple kinds and layers of meaning in each situation are uncovered. For unlearners in their twenties, the eleventh vignette, in which one falls in love with someone from a culture poorly regarded in one's own culture, has usually attracted the most interest—and most poignant tales. Unlearners from East Asian countries who have returned home from studying in America report that the situation in vignette twelve, in which one is perceived as having changed in undesirable ways from exposure to another culture, is an especially painful surprise.

2. *Three questions about culture.* Unlearners are asked to respond anonymously to this three-part exercise: Name something about a culture different from your own that you find (1) charming or amusing, (2) somewhat ridiculous, and (3) somewhat immoral or disgusting or that makes you angry. The answers are collected and collated, and the resulting set of all the answers is returned to the group as a whole. In multicultural groups of twenty to forty people, misunderstandings, prejudices, factual errors, and remarkably insensitive statements going in all directions are seen. No single race or culture or gender is immune. As a result, ethnocentricity is seen as an inner attitude to be changed rather than simply incorrect external knowledge. It becomes apparent that finding various cultural practices charming or amusing can be just as insensitive as finding them immoral or disgusting. The relativity of cultural practices is also clearly displayed, for the same practice will frequently be described by some respondents as charming and by others as ridiculous or infuriating.

3. *The cultural significance of personal names.* Members are asked to discuss in small groups the meaning in their own cultures of their first and last names. It turns out to be a subject that few have thought much about but that nearly everyone has some knowledge of. The discussion often shifts after a while to practices of naming

in various cultures. This exercise is especially useful for cross-cultural discussions between Westerners and East Asians, since each group has names that the other finds unfamiliar, hard to pronounce, often hard to remember, and literally meaningless until made more real by a discussion of the cultural meaning. In the process of this exercise, a wealth of fascinating facts about naming practices always emerges, even though this is not the main point of the exercise.

The specific questions I use are as follows:

- What does your name mean in your culture? Does it say that you are any special type of person (for example, strong, wise, beautiful, and so on)?

- What nicknames if any do you have? Are they nicknames that commonly go with your name (as, for example, *Bob* goes with *Robert*) or are they more peculiar to you personally?

- How common is your name? Is it found mainly in your culture, or is it found in other cultures as well?

- Does your name have any religious significance?

- Does your name have a clear gender association, that is, is it definitely masculine or feminine in your culture? Is there a variation of your name that is given to the opposite sex?

- Do you have any reminders that you tell people to help them remember your name?

- Is your name the subject of any songs or jokes in your culture? Are there children's rhymes that use your name?

- What else would you say about your name to help someone remember it and remember what it means?

4. *Linguicentrism.* This exercise builds on our unconscious assumption that we know how to speak our language, and that we have the right to judge the adequacy of another's attempts to speak it and to become irritated and impatient when we "decide" that other person is inadequate. The exercise is usually done with articles or cartoons that show people speaking or writing "fractured" versions of a particular language (in my sessions, English). Participants are allowed, even encouraged to "have a good laugh" at the bizarre locutions. For example:

- In a Copenhagen airline ticket office: "We take your bags and send them in all directions."

- In a Japanese hotel: "You are invited to take advantage of the chambermaid."

- In an Acapulco hotel: "The manager has personally passed all the water served here."

But then the question is posed of why we laugh at misconstructions like these. (Only those laugh, by the way, who have firsthand colloquial knowledge of the language. Those for whom English is a second or third language tend to miss the double entendres.) Unlearners come to see that their laughter rests on an unconscious assumption of the rightness of their own way of using the language, a feeling of superiority toward those who misconstruct or mispronounce it. This insight is crystallized in the term *linguicentrism*. Once introduced, the idea of linguicentrism turns out to have applications for unlearning in many cross-cultural situations.

5. *Cartoons and advertisements.* Cartoons and advertisements can serve as wonderful vehicles for studying context because both forms require an instantaneous grasp of context if we are to "get the point." In this exercise, once unlearners feel (through feeling learning) that they have gotten the point, that they know it in a deep way, then, through creative learning and reflexive learning, they

can deconstruct the context that they grasped and see how the various components of the cartoon or advertisement function as a system to create meaning. Cartoons and advertisements have two additional advantages. First, they are heavily visual and symbolic and thus powerfully make the point that meaning is far deeper and more complex than verbal definitions of it. Second, they tend to be culture-bound in their meaning—they are written within a given cultural framework to be understood by knowledgeable members of that culture. The mystification of those who do not have the cultural key provides a fruitful basis for discussion of cultural differences. Cartoons that are from different cultures but about the same world events and advertisements that are from different cultures but about the same products can also often produce powerful unlearning experiences as unlearners discover how context changes the way events and products are understood.

6. *Condescension.* The phenomenon of talking down to others of different cultures, races, genders, ages, and so forth is a common problem in cross-cultural situations, including cross-cultural unlearning situations where various participants debate with each other over the meaning of various concepts, case problems, and hypothetical situations. Sometimes it pays to make condescension an object of reflection in its own right. What is going on in the phenomenon of condescension? When there are multiple language groups present, it is instructive to find the equivalent word or words that mean condescension in other languages, both the spoken and written forms. The word has multiple translations into East Asian languages, each with various subtleties of meaning. Making condescension problematic in its own right is an example of practicing phenomenological reduction—in this case, on an attitude that normally remains perniciously tacit in human communication.

7. *The contexts of physical objects.* Every man-made object, from a pencil or a comb to a skyscraper or a theme park is both a context for other actions and an event with its own context, which gives it meaning. This truth can be demonstrated by inviting unlearners to

examine various obviously man-made objects whose intended use is not clear (old tools from antique stores are good). As unlearners theorize about the intended use, they come to realize that what they are doing is a laborious step-by-step replication of a process that is normally instantaneous and unconscious as a result of cultural training, namely, the process of constructing context. The instantaneous process occurs when we look at a pencil. It does not occur when we look at an eighteenth-century tool for leather working or some space-age electronic device. But we can theorize and theorize richly, and in so doing, unlearners come to see how they use contextual clues of various kinds all the time to impute meaning to things.

A variation is to place a collection of objects of the same generic kind in front of a group of unlearners and ask group members to discuss the contexts that make one item or another appropriate or inappropriate. The exercise works very well using the briefcases that unlearners have brought with them into the room. Some are "upscale" and some distinctly are not; some are "old" and some are "new"; some are "masculine" and some are "feminine"; some mean "intellectual" and some mean "dilettante." People immediately agree on a meaning for some of the objects but vigorously debate others, leading to the idea that some contexts are more equivocal than others. Eyeglasses also work well for this exercise, as do shoes. Once again, reflection (reflexive learning) on the meaning of everyday objects draws unlearners into regions of questioning and creative learning that they often had never imagined existed.

8. *Definitions and cross-cultural accountability.* Commonly in cross-cultural conversations, we find it necessary to define our terms. In particular, the various "isms"—racism, sexism, ageism, and the like—often cry out for definition. Creative and expressive learning about definitions can be achieved by asking unlearners to write down the best definition they can create for one of the isms, and then take that definition to another group member who is the object or the practitioner of that particular kind of bigotry. A male unlearner takes his definition of sexism to a female unlearner, for example. The two

of them then have a discussion about the definition. The unlearning lies in discovering how much of the other person's experience may not have been captured in the carefully wrought definition. The conversations that the unlearners have tend to be quite powerful experiences. One woman unlearner had a five-hour conversation with her father about her definition of sexism and said later that it was the longest sustained interaction she had ever had with him.

9. *Measuring cultural synergy.* A group of unlearners is given the task of coming up with a way of measuring the degree of cultural synergy present in a group. *Cultural synergy* is defined as the capacity of a group or organization to conduct itself in such a way that all the cultural perspectives and resources of the various members of the group are combined on behalf of the group's pursuit of its objectives and, further, that the *way* of combining the resources and perspectives has an enhancing effect on each resource and perspective taken individually.

This task requires all of the qualities of learning as a way of being. If it becomes merely a passive intellectual analytical task, participants will quickly feel it growing sterile and mechanistic and will lose interest. Feeling learning is a particularly important quality in this task. Participants find themselves reflecting deeply on what true synergy feels like when it is present and what it feels like when it is absent. The task is most effectively performed when participants realize that they can use the assignment to learn things about the degree of synergy or lack of it present in the group—in other words, when they convert the task into an inquiry conducted through self-directed learning, rather than seeing it as a search for "the right answer."

10. *Uncovering tacit knowledge.* Throughout this chapter, I have frequently referred to the commonsense, unstated, taken-for-granted aspects of culture. *Tacit knowledge* is a good phrase for all this taken-for-granted material. How does one know how to bow in Japan; how to shake hands in the West; when it is all right to call someone by his or her first name; when it is accurate to say in a restaurant that the service is slow; what accessories go with a particular suit or dress;

how much is too much for a tip to a waiter, bellhop, or cab driver; why a joke is funny; and so forth ad infinitum? Every culture is composed of countless facts and methods whereby problems are solved, interpretations are made, and courses of action are taken "without thinking about it."

Unlearners can be asked to keep journals and to interact with each other over an extended period of time to observe and discuss tacit knowledge. If it is a multicultural group, the participants can trigger each other's thinking by asking naïve questions of each other about cultural practices. One exciting variation is to hold these discussions in cyberspace, so people can post their observations asynchronously and post reactions to each other's observations. The computer introduces a slight degree of impersonality which, in an interesting way, seems to free people to ask questions and express opinions about things—for example, sexual practices—that they might be hesitant to discuss face to face (and thus it increases expressive learning). The fact that the postings are written out is important, too, because that gives unlearners an opportunity to reflect on each other's comments and questions (and thus increases reflexive learning). Finally, a computer conference can continue for an indefinite period of time, enabling unlearners to probe more deeply into the tacit knowledge of their own and each other's cultures (and it thus encourages continual learning).

Conclusion

I have explored two approaches to cultural unlearning. First, I examined a method for becoming more aware of the mentality we bring into situations, with the objective of seeing how our mentality conditions what we can see and understand there. Second, I introduced the idea that we can learn to understand contexts, that is, stop taking for granted the taken-for-granted. Both of these methods are forms of unlearning—the letting go of previous learnings in order to open ourselves to new learnings.

The ten activities at the end of the chapter exemplify the kinds of things that can be done to stimulate cultural unlearning as a way of being. I do not offer them as the "best" but rather as illustrations of how to get beyond institutional learning philosophy and practice when we consider cross-cultural situations.

I employed the term *unlearning* to underscore the basic point about understanding cross-cultural relationships: the main work required is work we do on ourselves in relation to our own familiar cultures. The philosophy of institutional learning misleads us when it tells us that we need do no work on ourselves and that our focus should be on other cultures rather than our own. We have the rest of our lives to learn specific mentalities and styles of other cultures. Our preparation for this cultural learning as a way of being is unlearning of the kind discussed in this chapter.

· · · · · · ·

Of all the many kinds of cultural differences, differences in deep values, worldviews, and matters of faith are among the most difficult to understand, accept, and deal with. Even for those within a single culture—and certainly for those within the North American culture—the topics of spirituality and religion may not be easy to discuss. Yet, perception of the particular spiritual nature of a culture may be one of the most important cultural keys to understanding it and continual learning and growth on this topics may be the most important kind of learning we can do in permanent white water. Spiritual learning, therefore, is appropriately the last form of learning as a way of being that I discuss.

6

. . . .

Spiritual Learning

During the period that the ideas in this book were developed and the book written, tumult seemed loosed in the world as we in the United States knew it. From the Gulf War to Bosnia to Chechnya; from Lebanon to Rwanda to Oklahoma City; from Rodney King to O. J. Simpson to Susan Smith; from "gays in the military," to Gennifer Flowers, to health care reform, to Vincent Foster, to Whitewater; from "barbarians at the gate" to the *Exxon Valdez* to massive layoffs and downsizing everywhere—responsible managerial leaders and observers of their work have been buffeted daily with shocks, horrors, and absurdities beyond even the "normal" level of post–World War II turbulence and change. Moreover, the horror and pain that is embodied in many of these events is not their only characteristic, maybe not even their most significant characteristic. For they have also in common that they go abruptly, violently, absurdly outside the prevailing value system, that they were almost unimaginable to the general public when they occurred. A generation ago, Herman Kahn used thermonuclear war as his image of "unthinkability" (Kahn, 1962). Today, unthinkability is much closer to home, embedded in daily experience. Managerial leadership in permanent white water entails continually thinking about and acting wisely toward the unthinkable.

I said in the Introduction that permanent white water creates "a felt lack of continuity, a felt lack of direction, absence of a sense of progress, absence of a feeling of cumulative achievement, a lack of coherence, a feeling of meaninglessness, and a lack of control. Clearly, permanent white water is not just facts and events surrounding members of organizations. Permanent white water is the meaning we as system members attach to our experiences.

Another word for permanent white water is *confusion*—the problem of what to believe; whom to trust; what events, technologies, groups and organizations, and laws and traditions can serve as anchors of meaning. In the modern world, meaninglessness derives not only from an absence of sources of meaning but, ironically, also from a surfeit, a cacophony of competing meanings as offered by this or that guru, this or that "total system," this or that self-improvement program. The incredible variety of competing sources of potential meaning acts back on our consciousness, adding to the confusion we feel. We often hear criticism that people tend to go from one "solution" to another, to jump from bandwagon to bandwagon without ever touching solid ground. But it is important that we understand why this is so.

My perception is that managerial leaders of the past several decades have been among the most energetic and conscientious of those seeking to maintain and enhance the meaning of their lives and the lives of others in the face of all the confusion created by permanent white water. After all, the managerial leader's *job* is to maintain and enhance the organization as a meaningful place. More and more, as white water increases, leadership consists precisely in leading in the creation of new meanings, new grounds and reasons for the organization to be doing what it is doing, new understandings of the torrents of change that inundate us. This is how men and women who are managerial leaders attempt to face unthinkability and help others face it too. But the pressure on them is enormous. In George Macdonald's poignant words: "It is hardly to be wondered at that he should lose the finer consciousness of higher powers and deeper feelings, not from any behavior in itself wrong, but from the hurry, noise, and tumult in the streets of life, that, penetrating too deep into the house of life, dazed and stupefied the silent and lowly watcher in the chamber of conscience, far apart. He had no time to think or feel" (Quoted in Tileston, 1934, p. 238).

Spirituality as a Source of Meaning

In this chapter, I take it as a given that in times of confusion, fear, loss, and doubt, human beings turn to transcendent sources of meaning for succor and reinspiration. Of course we do other things as well: we deny that things are as bad as they seem, or we increase the intellectual intensity of our analysis of our problems, or we redouble our efforts to make the world "behave," or we bond more tightly together in familiar groupings seeking succor from each other, or we find scapegoats for our problems in the actions of other human beings and seek to exterminate them, or we seek more tranquil venues where the troubles of the world cannot (we hope) reach us, or we place our trust in leaders who promise to alleviate our suffering, or, as Socrates noted long ago, we become philosophers.

I do not undertake a critique of any of these methods or the many others we can invent but, instead, simply note that every worldly action or system intended to alleviate the cosmic pain of meaninglessness is subject itself to the same disease. One alternative is to try to get beyond worldly solutions, and it is this impulse that grounds the contemporary interest in spirituality in organizational life. *Spirituality* is a decision to search somewhere else than in findings defined as scientific and their derived practices, in secular support systems, in positive addictions like aerobic exercise, or in any other man-made doctrines and technologies that purport to offer answers. Spirituality seeks fundamentally to get beyond materialist conceptions of meaning.

Spirituality is a decision to search beyond what one can do *to* or *on* or *within* oneself. Spirituality perceives the inadequacy to lie fundamentally not in material props but in the self that would do the propping. Thus, to be spiritual is to turn away from material props and to open oneself to a transcendent source of meaning. Of course, here, at this act of opening, is where all the theological and religious debates of human history *begin*. This chapter is not going to resolve these debates. It can only locate them and underline their relevance to organizational life and the work of managerial leaders.

To call this turning away from the material props a *search*, and to see that search as conducted by an individual, results in a view of spirituality as a personal process, occurring over time and expressing at each moment the person's sense of the meaning of life, of what the important questions are, of the significance of the persons and things around him or her, and of the direction that his or her journey is taking. To call spirituality a personal process means that inevitably debates will occur, for no two of us have the same needs for meaning nor will we seek to open ourselves to the transcendent in quite the same way. But these debates can be dialogue, as theologians seem increasingly to have discovered over the past quarter century and as organizations in the world of work are also discovering (Bohm, 1985). Debate over spirituality does not need to be a matter of win-lose communication. We know that the end of that road is persecutions, religious wars, profound hatreds, and destruction of spiritual consciousness itself. None of this impugns spirituality, of course, only our tendency to fall back into the material ways of the world to prop up our spiritual discoveries and realizations.

Genuine spirituality, then, is the willingness to enter into a process of dialogue about meaning, within oneself and with others; to stay with it over a period of time; and to remember that so far, no one has found the compelling once-and-for-all answer that warrants enforced universal adherence, the doctrines of several world religions notwithstanding. Rather than debate the absolutes of who is right, we all need to learn to think and communicate more theologically—something, however, that is probably not presently contemplated for any known M.B.A. curriculum or corporate management development program. Willingness to discuss spirituality is a mentality that becomes increasingly important, though, as more and more people embark on their own spiritual searches rather than accept "off the shelf" a given body of doctrine.

The Re-Creation of Spirituality

To speak matter-of-factly of spirituality as an ongoing search for meaning is perhaps to pay too little attention to the buffeting spirituality itself is taking in the white water of the modern world. After all, for millions of people, the traditional sources of spiritual awareness in organized religion have also lost meaning and are no longer trusted or taken seriously. It is entirely possible that, obvious and widespread as the need for renewed meaning is, the so-called spiritual realm is not seen by many people as a fruitful place to look. Spiritual awareness is not something that is today easily inherited. The family and the community church, as traditional institutions that bred spiritual faith and spiritual practice in childhood, may no longer be playing that role as effectively as they once did. The public school system is thoroughly secularized. In North America, the hegemony of the Judeo-Christian tradition itself has been reduced by the rise of spiritual traditions other than those traditionally found in Euro-American society. The inculcation of faith and belief is itself in white water. In the long run, these may be salutary trends, but in the shorter run, individuals may be less likely to possess from childhood an inner feeling for the spiritual and to know how to engage themselves in a process of spiritual development.

And so, once again, I come back to the learning process as a critical but neglected component in our lives. The spiritual search that permanent white water has made so imperative is a powerful instance of learning as a way of being. Conversely, the learning challenges of spiritual search are probably not going to be solved by the methods of institutional learning with its emphasis on expert control, indoctrination, conformity, the one right answer, the irrelevance of community among learners, and suppression of attention to the inner experience of learning.

But how do we know that there is something to search for, that there is learning available? There have been many answers and interpretations over the millennia. To me, one of the most persuasive is Paul Tillich's, for he was concerned with precisely the conditions of modern life that make up permanent white water. In his extraordinary meditation on the spiritual significance of anxiety and meaninglessness, *The Courage to Be*, Tillich (1952) came to what I regard as a most heartening conclusion. The struggle with the unthinkability of the modern condition, the willingness to keep getting back in the boat and shooting the next set of rapids, is fundamentally an act of spiritual affirmation. As Tillich says:

> Courage participates in the self-affirmation of being-itself, it participates in the power of being which prevails against nonbeing. . . . Man is not necessarily aware of this source. In situations of cynicism and indifference he is not aware of it. But it works in him as long as he has the courage to take his anxiety upon himself. In the act of the courage to be the power of being is effective in us, whether we recognize it or not. Every act of courage is a manifestation of the ground of being, however questionable the content of the act may be. The content may hide or distort true being, the courage in it reveals true being. Not arguments but the courage to be reveals the true nature of being itself. By affirming our being we participate in the self-affirmation of being-itself. There are no valid arguments for the "existence" of God, but there are acts of courage in which we affirm the power of being, whether we know it or not. If we know it, we accept acceptance consciously. If we do not know it, we nevertheless accept it and participate in it. And in our acceptance of that which we do not know the power of being is manifest in us. Courage has revealing power, the courage to be is the key to being-itself [1952, p. 181].

If Tillich is right, permanent white water is a blessing! It is our opportunity to rise above complacency and naïveté, to confront the deeper dilemmas of our existence, to be tempted by cynicism and negativity and despair, but to see finally the truth that lies beneath our frustration: "The act of accepting meaninglessness is in itself a meaningful act. It is an act of faith" (p. 176).

But "man is not necessarily aware of this source," says Tillich, that is, of the connection to being-itself. Perhaps the gradual forming and deepening of this awareness, of this connection to the ground of being, to the spirit, *is* the learning that permanent white water affords. The question is, what might that learning process look like? The core argument of this book is that the learning process should have the seven qualities of learning as a way of being—that it should be self-directed and creative, be variously expressive and certainly involve powerful feeling of meaning, occur on-line in the many walks of one's life and continually throughout one's life, and definitely provoke reflexive learning. In the present context, that reflexive learning is about spiritual development itself.

But what is the content of *spiritual learning as a way of being?* In considering systems thinking, leaderly thinking, and cultural unlearning, we are not moved to ask as we are so often with spiritual learning, "But what *is* it?" Tillich, I believe, would say that spiritual learning as a way of being is learning of the ways that our courageous daily struggles in white water connect us to the ground of being and ensure our participation in it. But is it possible to be more concrete than this?

Spirituality as Holistic Perception

When we say we genuinely "feel the spirit" in or of some entity, what are we saying? We are making a statement about a presence or current of energy or palpable intensity in the entity that goes beyond its existence and normal operation. We are not describing a force from outside but rather an intrinsic characteristic that has become manifest to us. We are not saying that the entity's "normal" reality and operation has no meaning but instead that we are seeing its normal meaning as profoundly enhanced, enriched, strengthened, and intensified by this spirit that we feel. We know we can have this experience of spirit inhering in all kinds of entities: in families; in sports teams; in institutions like schools, hospitals, armies, and corporations; in processes (when we speak of the spirit of inquiry, of the law, or of creativity, for example); in works of art and artistic processes; in individual persons (when we see deeply into the meaning of someone's life, for example); in the bonds of loyalty and love between individuals; and in nature, both as concrete systems and events and as abstract laws and relationships. In short, as humans we are capable of seeing and feeling the spirit in virtually anything.

When we have these clear perceptions of the spirit "in" people and things, I believe we are seeing them in their essence. We are experiencing *holistic perception*. We are grasping all at once the details of their operations, their histories, their effects, their human significance. We are seeing them whole. Our learning about them has moved our awareness beyond their component parts and beyond their problems and instabilities. We are experiencing the beauty and the goodness running all through them, inhering in their essence. We are letting ourselves feel wonder, awe, and astonishment. The effect on us is frequently physical: we tear up and speak chokingly, we have to get up and move, we suck our breath in and tremble.

When we have these perceptions, we do not doubt them or try to fight them off or jump into an analytic mode of minutely examining just exactly what it is that we think we see. The perception of the whole may not last very long, but we do not willingly destroy it.

In speaking this way, I am not making the metaphysical claim that there is spirit and beauty and goodness in all things, although one could certainly believe that. Rather I am making a contingent and empirical statement: *when* we see something whole, we see beauty and goodness and spirit. I am also pointing to the interesting fact that people regularly have these perceptions in relation to all sorts of things and to other people in their experience. (Of course, we may also see something evil when we see something whole, which is perhaps how the idea of evil spirits gains its credence.) The learning is there to be had. We can learn to appreciate spirit, and that learning process is, for me, spirituality.

Interesting implications follow from this way of talking. For one thing—which should come as a great relief to those with a modern critical intelligence that likes facts and methods—our spirituality does not have to *start* with a cosmic-level postulate of (big "S") Spirit. Our belief that we must start out with a fully realized vision of God or Spirit or the Divine is a holdover from medieval times, when the Church's primary organizational objective was to exert control in the face of chaotic political and economic conditions. There are still strong echoes of control in organized religion, of course, but there is also plenty of evidence that a person's spiritual search does not need to *start* with the turning over of his or her intelligence and will to a religious hierarchy. There are plenty of religious and other spiritual groupings and doctrines whose primary objective is support and liberation of the human spirit rather than control of it.

Another very significant implication of spirituality as holistic perception is its dynamism. There need be no limit on the number of different kinds of things we may perceive in spiritual terms. We do not have to divide up the world into spiritual things and non-spiritual things. As Tillich says, the *content* of an act of courage is not the point; that it *is* an act of courage in the face of meaninglessness and absurdity is what we should focus on in order to see its spiritual basis.

Furthermore, the *scale* of the things we are perceiving holistically is unlimited. We do not have to start with a cosmic awareness, but perhaps we can learn our way to one, so to speak. Indeed, it may be just here that one of the most destructive consequences of institutional learning–based indoctrination manifests itself. How can we have a deep understanding of and faith in spiritual truths when we have been forced to learn them in ways that are untrue to our own spirit? No wonder that for so many millions of people religious matters are either things one accepts as true but does not try to think very much about day to day or are matters of anguished questioning, hairsplitting, and rebellion. In neither case do we experience the "peace that passeth understanding," which supposedly is the whole point of spirituality. A spirituality that is learned and developed in a way true to the human spirit, that is, as part of learning as a way of being, has a much better chance, I believe, of bringing with it the comfort, serenity, and faith that we seek.

Permanent White Water and Spiritual Integrity

Much as we value our holistic perceptions and the spirit that we feel in them, we have to let them be the evolving, changing things that they are. In an earlier essay (Vaill, 1990, p. 349), I suggested the phrase "progressive transcendence" to capture the idea and quality of continual movement to larger and deeper appreciations of spiritual presence. At the time, I was thinking of the process as essentially voluntary, but I am now not so sure that it is or should be. If we do not progressively transcend our holistic perceptions, there is the danger that we will become fixated on specific perceptions. The twentieth century has seen some notably lamentable fixations—on race, blood, nation, profession, turf, ideology, family, gender, and so forth—where what started out as a deep perception of the spiritual integrity of some group or process or place or thing turned into a siege mentality in which the thing-as-perceived came to demand allegiance and defense at all costs.

But systems thinking teaches us that there are no closed systems. Our perception of spiritual integrity cannot be a closed system, much as we might cherish the object of our awareness and wish to protect it against all forms of white water. The white water, however, is existential. It can not be prevented from calling meanings into question, from opening new possibilities before us, possibilities that may be experienced as beckoning opportunity or yawning abyss.

Over the course of this book, I have perhaps treated permanent white water more as yawning abyss than as beckoning opportunity. However, in light of the theme of perceived spiritual integrity that may progressively transcend itself, we can see white water not as a disruptive horror but as the creative source of continued spiritual growth. Managerial leaders are expected to supply bold vision that will help lift others and bear them through the turbulent and frustrating currents of white water. We hope such leaders will be able to contribute to the esprit of the system they are leading. What does it mean to be able to remain inspired in the midst of all the difficulties of permanent white water? Is it reasonable to expect that managerial leaders can learn to do this? A study I conducted in 1994 supplies positive evidence that inspirational leadership has not yet itself been inundated by the torrents of change. Thirty-five experienced executives were given the task of writing a case study of the best white water managerial leader they had ever worked with. They were not to write about celebrities but about men and women they had observed firsthand. They were both to describe how these leaders worked and to draw such conclusions as they could about the personal qualities these individuals seemed to possess.

A fascinating array of individuals was described, from all walks of life. The cases contained many memorable scenes of leaders navigating organizational, technological, economic, and political white water of the most extreme kind. However, when it came to the question of the personal qualities that seemed to make the most difference, there was a striking degree of consensus, even though the thirty-five writers had not consulted with each other in forming their conclusions. Two qualities of the effective white water leader were mentioned over and over again, both of which are also amply supported in the research literature on effective management. One quality was the ability to stay with a clear mission and purpose, despite the most intense and continual drenching with the imperatives of daily crises and disasters, and to articulate this clarity continually to all those involved. These effective leaders would not permit organizational members to be panicked into thinking in small short-term survival terms. The second quality was what many study participants independently called "inclusiveness"—the ability to keep members of the organization in touch with each other, to help people feel needed and significant, to combat people's feelings of being cut off and isolated and the resentment that white water often causes. In the way the participants described this ability, it was clear that it went beyond merely providing information and occasions for people to stay in contact. It included communicating with *feeling* the leader's deep conviction of the importance of staying together and of supporting each other. It is not an exaggeration in many of the cases to say that the leader expressed love for the members of the system and helped them to love each other.

I believe that these cases are filled with a positive note that integrates the major themes of this book: the reality and persistence of the white water, the need for managerial leaders to learn more effectively to cope with its effects, and the possibility that living and working in white water actually sharpens and strengthens leaders' ability and determination to stay in touch with the spirit that runs through our organizations and our lives. Learning as a way of being is a personal search for the spirit of the permanent white water.

Epilogue

· ·

Discovery, Cultivation, Recognition, and the Real Learnings of Life

You are a corporate recruiter looking over the transcripts of a very promising young job applicant. There are two things that you note—that in fact you would note on the great majority of transcripts of young persons who came to your attention as potential hirees for management and professional positions: first, you see a pattern of good grades, averaging out on the undergraduate transcript to 3.2 and on the master's degree transcript to 3.7. You see very few C's and no D's or F's. You note summer school courses on both transcripts; these undergraduate summer courses enabled the applicant to finish the initial degree in three and one-half years.

The second thing you notice is that the majority of the courses the person took after the sophomore year have very practical-sounding titles. There are lots of business words in these titles—words like "accounting" and "finance" and "information systems" and "organizations." These business words are modified by phrases like "advanced problems in" or "current issues in" or "modern approaches to." You note two or three courses that seem to be about human behavior and a couple with "leadership" in the title. There is one course about "managing stress" and "effective self-care." Another seems to deal with international trends of various kinds. All in all, you seem to be looking at the transcripts of a very bright and capable young person who is firmly focused on a professional career in a corporation and has obviously tried to make as much use as possible of the college years to prepare for such a career.

. . . .

I suggest, however, in keeping with the themes of this book, particularly as developed in Chapter Four, that in this scenario you really know very little about how well prepared this person is for managerial leadership, or even for embarking on a managerial apprenticeship, in your corporation or in any other setting for that matter. The transcript does not provide any evidence of what the person can *do*, but of course that has always been true of transcripts. Nor does the transcript provide any evidence of the person's fundamental qualities of character, but that, too, has always been invisible on transcripts. However, beyond those two deficiencies, which you are accustomed and resigned to, the transcript does not tell you anything about the person as a *learner*.

The transcript does not tell you about the person's capacity to frame a problem or conduct a process of inquiry. It does not reveal whether the person has much capacity to engage in dialogue with others for mutual enlightenment. It does not tell you whether the person has a broad or a narrow view of life. The transcript certainly does not tell you how self-aware the person is as a learner nor does it gauge how much respect for himself or herself as a learner the person has. The A's and B's do not discriminate between the courses that were full of surprise and delight for the person and those whose requirements the person met equally well but without much élan or personal involvement. In fact, for all you know, *none* of those A's and B's were earned in a mood of élan and delight.

Of course, there are other methods of assessing this young person's ability and potential, and many of them may address the questions implied here. But the transcripts themselves do not tell you much that is relevant to life in the organizational world of permanent white water. A transcript is, in fact, an impoverished document. If it were only the document that were impoverished, there would be no cause for concern, but I believe that this impoverished document symbolizes an impoverished educational experience in which all the emphasis has been on filling the mental bucket with as much impersonal information as possible. The learning abilities that you, a potential employer, would like to be assured have been part of this young person's development have not been encouraged. These qualities are not only not valued in institutional learning, they are not even understood. There are no educational systems in place to foster them. There is no institutional attention to doing a better job of fostering them. There is no mission to produce *learners*. The mission is to produce *graduates*, as measured by some fixed amount of information correctly regurgitated on examinations and term papers.

As Chittister notes in her wonderful little commentary on the Rule of St. Benedict:

> Benedict teaches life is a learning process. Western culture and its emphasis on academic degrees, however, has almost smothered this truth. We have made the words "graduation" and "education" almost synonymous. We measure achievement in academic credits. We discount experience, depth, and failure. We believe in action and results and products and profits and youth, so we come to regard the elderly as essentially useless.
>
> But in the end, all of that kind of achievement is nothing but a spiritual wasteland if along the way we have not attached ourselves to the discovery of truth, the cultivation of beauty, and the recognition of the real learnings of life [1991, p. 24].

"Discovery," "cultivation," "recognition"—those are process words. They are names for ways of working, thinking, and feeling. They are all qualities of learning as a way of being. They apply to every subject, not just to things that a managerial leader needs to know. Anyone who knows something about discovery, cultivation, and recognition is in command of his or her learning processes and knows how to engage in learning as a way of being. Anyone who has only had discoveries presented to him or her, has only been exposed to already cultivated knowledge, and has never had any original cognitions on which true recognitions must be based is the recipient of a typical college and graduate school education and is unprepared to function in the world of permanent white water.

What has gone wrong? That is far too big a question for this book, although, happily, it is a question that educators are asking with increasing insistence. This book, though, can suggest one place to look for what has gone wrong, or perhaps I should say for what has been wrong all along. For there is one more thing to be said about the philosophy and practice of institutional learning, something that may be more fundamental than most of the concerns expressed in Chapter One. *Institutional learning assumes there is something to teach, separate and apart from the learner.* The philosophy of institutional learning performs an odd and extremely subtle piece of abstraction. It presumes that knowledge—all knowledge of whatever kind—can be structured coherently outside the human mind. It presumes that knowledge does not depend on the human mind for its embodiment and its organization. In this view, a textbook (or a CD-ROM) is just as real and valid an embodiment of knowledge as a master teacher speaking from memory and personal experience about the same material. This assumption has empowered institutional learning to occupy itself with efficient methods of transmitting the preexisting stock of knowledge to the learner and with developing methods to enforce that transmission over any characteristics in the learner or the surrounding world that might get in the way.

I suggest that behind this assumption of the independent existence of knowledge is a complex metaphysical conclusion. Philosophers still debate whether knowledge can exist outside the mind, but educators are clear that it can, and have forgotten that there is even a question! Knowledge, for most educators and certainly for the institutional learning system, exists outside the mind. It is distinct from the learner. The teacher's job is to organize it for the learner, present it, and test to make sure it has been successfully implanted. The primary operative objective is not to help the learner discover, cultivate, and recognize; it is to instruct the learner in (to structure in) existing discoveries, cultivations, and recognitions.

What would the opposite assumption be? That all knowledge is learner dependent? If that is so, the primary problem is not imparting knowledge to the learner but rather helping the learner to find his or her way to the knowledge. Just because we want two learners to learn the same multiplication table, we should not assume it should be taught to them in the same way. They might find their ways to it quite differently and, indeed, might hold it differently in mind all their lives, even though agreeing that two times two is four. If there might be differences in learners' paths for the simplest, most unequivocal kinds of knowledge, how much more difference in pathways might exist for complex concepts and for issues requiring the exercise of personal judgment? In training learners to look for the right answer, as the institutional learning model does with such devastating efficiency, that model systematically destroys the learner's consciousness of alternative pathways to knowledge. The process has been going on for so many generations that tragically, the consciousness of millions of *teachers* has also been destroyed, and they no longer understand the possibility of multiple pathways—nor may they have much energy for rediscovering them.

If we take learning as a way of being seriously, we have to take the idea of multiple pathways to knowledge seriously. In Chapter Four, I discussed our need to understand the learning challenges of managerial leadership, suggesting that all the subject matter that managerial leaders are exposed to should be examined for its learning challenges. Now it is clear why this examination is so necessary: if we are going to help learners walk their own learning paths, the support formal education can give them lies in helping them prepare themselves for the learning challenges that various subject matter poses. This clearly goes beyond subject matter for managerial leaders. The rest of what we call higher education could engage in similar reflection. What are the learning challenges of Shakespeare? of Beethoven's Ninth Symphony? of the theory of relativity? Throughout the twentieth century, learners have had to struggle with Einstein's "thought experiments" as if they were the only road to the theory of relativity. How many physics teachers are helping learners experience their own thought experiments?

What, after all, does the *higher* in "higher education" apply to? In institutional learning, higher mainly means "more" and maybe "harder." But if the referent for higher is some quality of the mind and spirit, and not just the number of credits on a transcript, perhaps the word has to do with the capacity of the linked mind and the spirit to direct themselves in their learning and development. If it is our linked minds and spirits that direct our learning processes, then we have a better chance of maintaining our participation in those processes. We are no longer passive vessels being filled with facts and methods that exist apart from us. What would it mean, both personally and institutionally, if we could fully grasp the significance of physicist Roger Jones's remark that "I had come to suspect, and now felt compelled to acknowledge, that science and the physical world were products of human imagining—that we were not cool observers of that world, but its passionate creators. We were all poets and the world was our metaphor" (Jones, 1990, p. 1)?

Higher education is today overwhelmingly organized on the principle that we are cool observers. Yet each of us, in his or her own learning as a way of being, knows the ways in which he or she is a passionate creator, whether anyone else recognizes it or not. Emerson says somewhere, "If a man does not write his poetry, it escapes by other vents from him" (and from a woman, too, I am sure he would agree). We all produce poems and prayers in various ways, and they are our passionate creations. Are not these passionate creations, conceived as we feel our way down the wild rivers of experience, truly higher than anything institutional learning can imagine?

Resource I

. . . .

Change Assessment Inventory

Peter Vaill and Eric Dent

Listed below are some general categories of importance to managerial leaders. You may or may not have noticed change in each category in recent years. For each category, please check the point on the scale that matches your own sense of the degree of change that has occurred. There are no objective answers for most of these items. What are sought are your subjective impressions. For your time horizon, pick a point in the past *at least three and no more than eight years ago*. Indicate here the number of years chosen: _____ .

Categories of Change

1. Your budget

____ Much looser	-3	____ A little tighter	+1
____ Somewhat looser	-2	____ Somewhat tighter	+2
____ A little looser	-1	____ Much tighter	+3
____ No change	0		

2. Professional employee qualifications

____ Much lower	-3	____ A little higher	+1
____ Somewhat lower	-2	____ Somewhat higher	+2
____ A little lower	-1	____ Much higher	+3
____ No change	0		

3. Deadlines

____ Much looser	-3	____ A little tighter	+1
____ Somewhat looser	-2	____ Somewhat tighter	+2

| ____ A little looser | -1 | ____ Much tighter | +3 |
| ____ No change | 0 | | |

4. Support from higher levels of management

____ Much more	-3	____ A little less	+1
____ Somewhat more	-2	____ Somewhat less	+2
____ A little more	-1	____ Much less	+3
____ No change	0		

5. Government regulations

____ Much less complex	-3	____ A little more complex	+1
____ Somewhat less complex	-2	____ Somewhat more complex	+2
____ A little less complex	-1	____ Much more complex	+3
____ No change	0		

6. Unexpected interruptions

____ Many fewer	-3	____ A little more	+1
____ Somewhat fewer	-2	____ Somewhat more	+2
____ A little fewer	-1	____ Much more	+3
____ No change	0		

7. Nonprofessional staff qualifications

____ Much lower	-3	____ A little higher	+1
____ Somewhat lower	-2	____ Somewhat higher	+2
____ A little lower	-1	____ Much higher	+3
____ No change	0		

8. Technological complexity

____ Much less	-3	____ A little greater	+1
____ Somewhat less	-2	____ Somewhat greater	+2
____ A little less	-1	____ Much greater	+3
____ No change	0		

9. Competition for resources

____ Much less	-3	____ A little greater	+1
____ Somewhat less	-2	____ Somewhat greater	+2
____ A little less	-1	____ Much greater	+3
____ No change	0		

10. Rate things are changing

_____ Much slower	-3	_____ A little faster	+1
_____ Somewhat slower	-2	_____ Somewhat faster	+2
_____ A little slower	-1	_____ Much faster	+3
_____ No change	0		

11. Ambitiousness of objectives

_____ Much less	-3	_____ A little greater	+1
_____ Somewhat less	-2	_____ Somewhat greater	+2
_____ A little less	-1	_____ Much greater	+3
_____ No change	0		

12. Time spent in meetings

_____ Much less	-3	_____ A little more	+1
_____ Somewhat less	-2	_____ Somewhat more	+2
_____ A little less	-1	_____ Much more	+3
_____ No change	0		

13. Racial/ethnic/gender diversity at work

_____ Much less	-3	_____ A little more	+1
_____ Somewhat less	-2	_____ Somewhat more	+2
_____ A little less	-1	_____ Much more	+3
_____ No change	0		

14. Adequacy of information for decisions

_____ Much better	-3	_____ A little poorer	+1
_____ Somewhat better	-2	_____ Somewhat poorer	+2
_____ A little better	-1	_____ Much poorer	+3
_____ No change	0		

15. Frequency of forced changes in organization's plans

_____ Much less often	-3	_____ A little more often	+1
_____ Somewhat less often	-2	_____ Somewhat more often	+2
_____ A little less often	-1	_____ Much more often	+3
_____ No change	0		

16. Changes in basic product or services

_____ Much less often	-3	_____ A little more often	+1
_____ Somewhat less often	-2	_____ Somewhat more often	+2

_____ A little less often   -1   _____ Much more often   +3

_____ No change   0

17. Amount of travel you do

_____ Much less   -3   _____ A little more   +1

_____ Somewhat less   -2   _____ Somewhat more   +2

_____ A little less   -1   _____ Much more   +3

_____ No change   0

18. Time spent dealing with difficult people

_____ Much less   -3   _____ A little more   +1

_____ Somewhat less   -2   _____ Somewhat more   +2

_____ A little less   -1   _____ Much more   +3

_____ No change   0

19. Frequency of novel, unprecedented problems

_____ Much less often   -3   _____ A little more often   +1

_____ Somewhat less often   -2   _____ Somewhat more often +2

_____ A little less often   -1   _____ Much more often   +3

_____ No change   0

20. Likelihood of a slowdown in rate of change

_____ Extremely likely   -3   _____ A little unlikely   +1

_____ Somewhat likely   -2   _____ Somewhat unlikely   +2

_____ A little likely   -1   _____ Extremely unlikely   +3

_____ No change   0

21. Overall stressfulness of your job

_____ Much less   -3   _____ A little greater   +1

_____ Somewhat less   -2   _____ Somewhat greater   +2

_____ A little less   -1   _____ Much greater   +3

_____ No change   0

Scoring

Your score is the net of the positive and negative numbers you have checked.

Follow-Up Questions

1. This questionnaire is designed to measure the extent to which you feel your work environment is becoming more dynamic, changing, unpredictable, and perhaps turbulent. Are there other factors in your work environment that are contributing either to increasing *instability* or to increasing *stability*? Please mention them briefly, noting which factors are contributing to instability and which to stability.

2. Using the same time horizon as you did for the previous questions, on balance, what word or phrase would you use to describe your attitude in your job over that period?

Resource II

∙ ∙

Exploration and Discovery:
A Dialogue of Learning

I composed the following fantasized dialogue after reading the journal accounts of thirty-five M.B.A. students, in which they described their attempts to understand the group processes of small task teams they had been members of. Most of the accounts expressed considerable frustration. The dominant theme was that they felt they did not know what they were supposed to be learning. At this time, I had also been reading Sir Francis Chichester's *Gypsy Moth Circles the World,* an account of his solo voyage during 1966 and 1967. After I had written the dialogue, I showed it to the students. Some of them saw the point of it, but many did not.

I am including this fantasized dialogue here because it displays some ideas about the nature of exploration and creativity that can help us better understand creative learning. Also it shows how a decision to employ a format that is unusual for me stimulated my own creativity.

I envisioned the group member in this dialogue as harried and somewhat distracted. The questions posed to Sir Francis are quite legitimate, though, and I respect the person for asking them, even

Note: This resource is a slightly edited version of my essay of the same title published in Exchange: The Organizational Behavior Teaching Journal (now Journal of Management Education), 1981, 6(2), pp. 15–19.

if in this imaginative work Sir Francis responds cryptically at times from his questioner's point of view.

GROUP MEMBER: Sir Francis, you have been extremely effective at setting and reaching difficult goals. I have some questions for you.

CHICHESTER: Yes?

GROUP MEMBER: I am pursuing a particular goal, together with a few friends of mine. We have spent much time on it and worked very hard. I feel we've made some progress, but I'm not sure we're doing the right thing. What's of even more concern to me is that I am not sure I'm learning what I am supposed to be learning as we work on this project. It is very important to me to accomplish something here because I have spent a considerable amount of money to have this experience and I have devoted a lot of time to it—more time than I ever expected I would, in fact.

CHICHESTER: Mmmmm.

GROUP MEMBER: So I want to know what I am supposed to be getting out of this experience.

CHICHESTER: I do not know how to get things out of experiences.

GROUP MEMBER: But you've been many places. You've done heroic things. Few men have faced death as often as you. Few have been forced to exercise every ounce of their ability, have been thrown back on their most basic resources, have had to innovate under the most extreme conditions. You must have learned something from these experiences.

CHICHESTER: Oh, indeed I have.

GROUP MEMBER: And furthermore, something must tell you what things you should be concentrating on and what things you can let go, what things to pay attention to and what things to ignore, in what areas you are vulnerable and in what areas you are relatively secure. In fact, from what little I know about the single-handed long-distance ocean sailing you do, it appears to me that you have to be tremendously skillful at planning and at preparing yourself and your boat. You've learned how to do these things so that you're more effective at reaching your goals than if you just casually decided on a Sunday afternoon to go off for a sail around the world. You certainly don't do that, do you?

CHICHESTER: No, indeed.

GROUP MEMBER: You do plan; you do have a goal?

CHICHESTER: Yes.

GROUP MEMBER: You do those things very well.

CHICHESTER: So I have heard.

GROUP MEMBER: Then how can you say you haven't learned from your experiences?

CHICHESTER: I didn't.

GROUP MEMBER: Well, okay, how to get things from experience . . . same thing.

CHICHESTER: Perhaps.

GROUP MEMBER: Then what is the key?

CHICHESTER: You seem to have a theory that I am a person-with-a-key. But what I am is an explorer.

GROUP MEMBER: I know, and a very good one. That's why I'm here.

CHICHESTER: Have you considered what it is to be an explorer?

GROUP MEMBER: Well, it's doing new things, and it can be dangerous and probably lonely and probably expensive. But people have always gone exploring, so it's obviously exciting and rewarding.

CHICHESTER: Yes, it is all those things. But have you considered what it is to be an explorer?

GROUP MEMBER: Besides the stuff I just mentioned?

CHICHESTER: Yes.

GROUP MEMBER: Well, it's probably emotional. I recall your writing about smashing your elbow when you were off the coast of Africa, for instance, and sailing a thousand miles with it inflamed and learning to drain fluid from it yourself and all. That was probably quite an emotional experience—it made very painful reading. It must have been terrible.

CHICHESTER: Yes, besides the pain, I was quite frightened that the elbow would become infected. That whole experience was exploration.

GROUP MEMBER: You mean you felt, "That's the breaks," as we Americans say?

CHICHESTER: No, I mean learning the anatomy and physiology of my elbow was exploration.

GROUP MEMBER: I'm not following you.

CHICHESTER: I know. Do you remember that my boat rolled through three hundred and sixty degrees off New Zealand?

GROUP MEMBER: That was about the most incredible thing I'd ever heard of—a sixty-foot boat rolling upside down and then rolling back up the other way.

CHICHESTER: That was quite an experience, too. The galley was a mess afterwards.

GROUP MEMBER: A lot of things happened that slowed you down from your goal.

CHICHESTER: That is what exploration is.

GROUP MEMBER: What is what exploration is?

CHICHESTER: My thought is that it is going forward while feeling very confused and uncertain as to where you are, where you're actually going forward to, and whether you have the resources to sustain you. You feel at best only partially in control of the situation and frequently not at all in control.

GROUP MEMBER: But you did achieve most of your goals. For instance, you may have been confused about where you were sometimes, but you were never lost. Didn't you hit Australia within ten miles or so of what you were aiming for after being out of sight of land for two months?

CHICHESTER: There is nothing extraordinary in that. Do you think I simply sailed the original course I set when I rounded Africa? If I'd done that and hit my destination within ten miles, it *would* have been extraordinary!

GROUP MEMBER: Well, what did you do?

CHICHESTER: Corrected course every day—at least, every day that I could see the sun or the stars.

GROUP MEMBER: All this isn't really telling me what I want to know.

CHICHESTER: That's because you still have not considered what it is to be an explorer who is constantly correcting course.

GROUP MEMBER: I wanted to ask you, though, why do you call yourself an explorer when you sail over courses that many others have sailed before?

CHICHESTER: Because *I* was exploring.

GROUP MEMBER: Oh, I see, you were exploring new ways to reach whatever port you were sailing to next! Now I think I am beginning to see what you mean. Searching for the better way, never being satisfied with existing knowledge, trying to add to what we know about long-distance single-handed passages, making sailing safer, developing techniques others can use. *I* see. It's the *way* I work in my group that I should pay attention to so that others who are learning about teamwork can benefit from my experiences. Thanks so much for your time. I've got the point now.

CHICHESTER: I am afraid you don't.

GROUP MEMBER: I don't? Well, what is it? Is it that you wrote a book about your experiences so others can learn from you? I should publish my research, you mean?

CHICHESTER: Well, writing a book is another kind of exploration.

GROUP MEMBER: Let me go back to something for a minute. Exploratively. Aren't you stretching the meaning of the word *explorer* a little when the goals you're seeking, the places you're trying to get to, have already been discovered by others? For instance, you *knew* what course to set for Western Australia when you rounded Africa.

CHICHESTER: Yes, I knew Western Australia was on that course.

GROUP MEMBER: Well, then, you're not really exploring. You decide what port you're going to sail to and then you sail there. But I don't know what port I'm trying to sail to. I don't even know if there *are* any ports in the direction I'm going. And if there are, I don't know if they're actually places I want to visit, and I don't want to waste my time and money finding out. That's the situation I'm in, and you can sit there puffing on your pipe and smiling at me if you want to, but you've already *done* your heroic deeds and all that. *I'm* the one who's hurting!!

CHICHESTER: You've gotten it.

GROUP MEMBER: What have I got?

CHICHESTER: You have gotten what it means to be an explorer.

GROUP MEMBER: Well, I don't like it, I can tell you—whatever it is I've got.

CHICHESTER: Then give it up.

GROUP MEMBER: I can't. We're past the Add/Drop period.

CHICHESTER: That must be what we call in voyaging the point of no return.

GROUP MEMBER: I wouldn't give it up anyway. That would be quitting. I'm committed in my mind to learning something.

CHICHESTER: Well, that's another part of what it means to be an explorer. The point of no return is not a place on a globe or a calendar; it's a place in the mind.

GROUP MEMBER: Okay. It's a place in the mind. Very wise. But still, when you rounded Africa, you *knew* Western Australia was there. It was fixed. It wasn't going to float away. Someone wasn't going to suddenly tell you half way there that you were going the wrong way.

CHICHESTER: No.

GROUP MEMBER: Well? Isn't that different from what I'm facing?

CHICHESTER: I once reached a port after a thirty-day passage to find it engulfed in a typhoon, with towering waves making any close approach certain disaster and a howling onshore wind driving me straight at it at maximum hull speed. What was my goal?

GROUP MEMBER: To get into the port?

CHICHESTER: To attempt to get into the port would have resulted in the certain destruction of my boat and my probable drowning. What was my goal?

GROUP MEMBER: To avoid your goal?

CHICHESTER: Just so.

GROUP MEMBER: But that's just a detail. Your real goal was to reach the port. You just had to delay the final approach for a while.

CHICHESTER: Perhaps, but that was small consolation then.

GROUP MEMBER: What happened?

CHICHESTER: I don't know. I was delirious with fever at the time. When next I became fully conscious, I was twenty miles away from the port. I don't know how I got there. It is even possible that there never was a storm, and I never did attempt an approach. But all this, too, is part of what it is to be an explorer.

GROUP MEMBER: I'm getting confused. Your goal was the port?

CHICHESTER: Yes.

GROUP MEMBER: You were clear about that?

CHICHESTER: Yes.

GROUP MEMBER: You'd been pursuing this goal for many days. All your navigating and your sailing skill and so on were aimed at attaining that goal?

CHICHESTER: Yes.

GROUP MEMBER: But that's precisely the situation I'm *not* in. I don't know what resources to organize in what way to reach what end. I don't have a "port."

CHICHESTER: Neither did I.

GROUP MEMBER: Well, true, you had to postpone the final step. But you had the port as a goal all along the way.

CHICHESTER: Let me try to say this in a way that will convey my feeling *as an explorer*. I did not have the port the way you insist that I had it along the way. What I had was a going-forward-toward. That going-forward-toward was a good deal more general than you imagine. It is the nonexplorers who rather naïvely assume that once they have a clear sharp picture in mind of where they are going, they can trust that picture through to the end. To be an explorer is to not know where, precisely and concretely, one is going. If that seems obscure, let me put it a slightly different way. The explorer feels your uncertainty and your fear and even sometimes your fury. However, he or she does not think these states of mind can be escaped. Instead, they are part of what the explorer explores. Perhaps that is the difference between the explorer and you; you want to avoid experiencing all these states of mind.

GROUP MEMBER: Going-forward-toward. Beats me.

CHICHESTER: When you go through your dark living room on

the way to the kitchen at 3 A.M., do you simply stride confidently across the floor?

GROUP MEMBER: Not unless I want to fall over the dog or crunch a toe on the coffee table.

CHICHESTER: What is your mind doing as you cross the room?

GROUP MEMBER: Feeling for the dog and the corner of the table.

CHICHESTER: Somewhat tentatively?

GROUP MEMBER: Yes.

CHICHESTER: Where is the kitchen, in your mind?

GROUP MEMBER: In my mind, it's . . . it's *there* but it's . . .

CHICHESTER: Somewhat subordinate to the more immediate concerns of the dog and the coffee table?

GROUP MEMBER: Yes, I guess so.

CHICHESTER: If you smelled a strong feces smell as you entered the darkened room, what would you do?

GROUP MEMBER: I would turn on the light.

CHICHESTER: For the obvious reason.

GROUP MEMBER: For the obvious reason.

CHICHESTER: The dog and the coffee table in turn become subordinate to yet a more immediate concern?

GROUP MEMBER: Yes. But I'm *still* trying to get to the kitchen.

CHICHESTER: Yes, you are still trying to get to the kitchen. You are going-forward-toward it. That is precisely the way a "port" is for me, right up to the point that I actually alight on the wharf. Meanwhile, along the way, as you say, a host of more immediate concerns occupy me, concerns with which I deal as best I can, sometimes neatly, but more often with the most precarious feeling of makeshift. That is what it is to be an explorer.

GROUP MEMBER [*Pause*]: Say, do you know Edmund Hillary?

CHICHESTER: Yes.

GROUP MEMBER: Could you put me in touch with him? I'm starting to feel that something like mountain climbing might give me a way to understand how to set and reach goals.

CHICHESTER [*Wearily*]: Possibly so.

References

Ackoff, R. L. *Redesigning the Future: A Systems Approach to Societal Problems.* New York: Wiley, 1974.

Argyris, C., and Schön, D. A. *Organizational Learning: A Theory of Action Perspective.* Reading, Mass.: Addison-Wesley, 1978.

Athos, A. G., and Gabarro, J. J. *Interpersonal Behavior: Communication and Understanding in Relationships.* Englewood Cliffs, N.J.: Prentice-Hall, 1978.

Axtell, R. E. *Do's and Taboos around the World.* New York: Wiley, 1993.

Back, K. W. *Beyond Words: The Story of Sensitivity Training and the Encounter Movement.* New York: Russell Sage Foundation, 1972.

Barber, B. *L. J. Henderson on the Social System.* Chicago: University of Chicago Press, 1970.

Barfield, O. *The Rediscovery of Meaning and Other Essays.* Middletown, Conn.: Wesleyan University Press, 1977.

Barfield, O. *Saving the Appearances.* Orlando, Fla.: Harcourt Brace Jovanovich, 1977. (Originally published 1957.)

Barnard, C. A. *The Functions of the Executive.* Cambridge, Mass.: Harvard University Press, 1938.

Barrett, W. *The Illusion of Technique.* New York: Doubleday, Anchor Books, 1978.

Bennis, W. G., Benne, K., and Chin, R. (eds.). *The Planning of Change.* Troy, N.Y.: Holt, Rinehart & Winston, 1961.

Bennis, W. G., and Nanus, B. *Leaders: The Strategies for Taking Charge.* New York: HarperCollins, 1985.

Bennis, W. G., and Schein, E. H. *Personal and Organizational Change Through Group Methods.* New York: Wiley, 1965.

Bernard, C. *Introduction to the Study of Experimental Medicine.* New York: Schuman, 1949. (Originally published 1927.)

Bohm, D. *Unfolding Meaning: A Weekend of Dialogue with David Bohm.* Loveland, Colo.: Foundation House, 1985.

Bradford, L. P., and others (eds.). *T-Group Theory and Laboratory Method*. New York: Wiley, 1964.

Brodkey, H. "Dying: An Update." *The New Yorker*, Feb. 7, 1994, pp. 70–84.

Burden, C. *Business in Literature*. Atlanta: Business Publications Division, Georgia State University College of Business Administration, 1988.

Cannon, W. B. *The Wisdom of the Body*. New York: W.W. Norton, 1939.

Cantor, N. *The Learning Process for Managers*. New York: HarperCollins, 1958.

Chichester, F. *Gypsy Moth Circles the World*. New York: Coward-McCann, 1968.

Chittister, J. *Wisdom Distilled from the Daily*. San Francisco: HarperSanFrancisco, 1990.

Churchill, W. S. *The Gathering Storm*. Boston: Houghton-Mifflin, 1948.

Clark, K. E., and Clark, M. B. *Choosing to Lead*. Charlotte, N.C.: Iron Gate Press, 1994.

Conrad, J. *Lord Jim*. New York: Random House, 1931. (Originally published 1900.)

Cross, E. Y., Katz, J. H., Miller, F. A., and Seashore, E. W. (eds.). *Promise of Diversity*. Homewood, Ill.: Irwin, 1994.

Dixon, N. M. *The Organizational Learning Cycle: How We Can Learn Collectively*. New York: McGraw-Hill, 1994.

Domling, W. "Program Notes" to *Symphony #4*, by Gustav Mahler. Sony Compact Disc SBK 46535, 1991.

Drath, W. H., and Paulus, C. J. *Making Common Sense*. Greensboro, N.C.: Center for Creative Leadership, 1994.

Emery, F. E. (ed.). *Systems Thinking: Selected Readings*. New York: Viking Penguin, 1969.

Ephron, N. Interview about the film *Sleepless in Seattle*. Showtime (cable television channel), June 15, 1994.

Fowler, H. W. *A Dictionary of Modern English Usage*. (2nd ed.) New York: Oxford University Press, 1965.

Gardner, J. W. *Self-Renewal*. New York: HarperCollins, 1964.

Ghiselin, B. (ed.). *The Creative Process*. New York: New American Library, 1952.

Hall, E. T. *Beyond Culture*. New York: Doubleday, Anchor Books, 1977.

Harris, M. *The Rise of Anthropological Theory*. New York: Crowell, 1968.

Heinlein, R. A. *Stranger in a Strange Land*. New York: Putnam, 1961.

Herzberg, F. *The Motivation to Work*. New York: Wiley, 1959.

Homans, G. *The Human Group*. Orlando, Fla.: Harcourt Brace, 1950.

Husserl, E. *The Crisis of European Sciences and Transcendental Phenomenology: An Introduction to Phenomenological Philosophy*. Evanston, Ill.: Northwestern University Press, 1970.

Illich, I. *Deschooling Society*. New York: HarperCollins, 1971.

Jones, R. S. *Physics as Metaphor*. Minneapolis: University of Minnesota Press, 1990.

Kahn, H. *Thinking About the Unthinkable*. New York: Horizon Press, 1962.

Kaplan, A. *New Worlds of Philosophy*. New York: Random House, 1961.

Kast, F. E., and Rosenzweig, J. E. *Organization and Management: A Systems Approach*. New York: McGraw-Hill, 1969.

Katz, D., and Kahn, R. L. *The Social Psychology of Organization*. New York: Wiley, 1966.

Keen, E. *A Primer in Phenomenological Psychology*. Lanham, Md.: University Press of America, n.d. (Originally published 1975.)

Knowles, M. E. *Informal Adult Education*. New York: Association Press, 1950.

Kolb, D. A. *Experiential Learning: Experience as a Source of Learning and Development*. Englewood Cliffs, N.J.: Prentice-Hall, 1984.

Lawson, H. *Reflexivity: The Postmodern Predicament*. London: Hutchinson, 1985.

McCall, M. W., Lombardo, M. M., and Morrison, A. M. *The Lessons of Experience*. Lexington, Mass.: Lexington Books, 1988.

McNair, M. P. (ed.). *The Case Method at the Harvard Business School*. New York: McGraw-Hill, 1954.

McNamara, R. S. *In Retrospect: The Tragedy and Lessons of Vietnam*. New York: Random House/Times Books, 1995.

Malinowski, B. *A Scientific Theory of Culture*. Chapel Hill: University of North Carolina Press, 1944.

Manz, C. C., and Sims, H. P. *Business Without Bosses*. New York: Wiley, 1993.

Maslow, A. H. *Motivation and Personality*. (2nd ed.) New York: HarperCollins, 1970.

Miller, D. (ed.). *Popper Selections*. Princeton, N.J.: Princeton University Press, 1985.

Oates, J. C. *The Profane Art: Essays and Reviews*. New York: Dutton, 1983.

Peters, T. J. *Thriving on Chaos*. New York: Knopf, 1987.

Polanyi, M. *Personal Knowledge: Towards a Post-Critical Philosophy*. New York: HarperCollins, 1964.

Porter, L. W., and McKibben, L. E. *Management Education and Development*. New York: McGraw-Hill, 1988.

Puffer, S. M. *Managerial Insights from Literature*. Boston: PWS-Kent, 1991.

Radcliffe-Brown, A. R. *A Natural Science of Society*. New York: Free Press, 1957.

Revans, R. W. "Action Learning and the Cowboys." *Organizational Development Journal*, Fall 1986, pp. 71–79.

Riesman, D. *The Lonely Crowd*. New Haven, Conn.: Yale University Press, 1950.

Roethlisberger, F. J., and Dickson, W. J. *Management and the Worker*. Cambridge, Mass.: Harvard University Press, 1939.

Roethlisberger, F. J., Lombard, G. F. F., and Ronken, H. *Training for Human Relations*. Boston: Harvard Business School Division of Research, 1954.

Rokeach, M. *The Open and Closed Mind*. New York: Basic Books, 1960.

Schön, D. A. *Beyond the Stable State*. New York: W.W. Norton, 1973.

Senge, P. M. *The Fifth Discipline*. New York: Doubleday, 1990.

Storr, A. *The Dynamics of Creation*. New York: Atheneum, 1972.

Suzuki, S. *Zen Mind, Beginner's Mind*. New York: Weatherhill, 1979.

Tileston, M. *Daily Strength for Daily Needs*. New York: Putnam, 1934.

Tillich, P. *The Courage to Be*. New Haven, Conn.: Yale University Press, 1952.

Trist, E. L., Higgin, G. W., Murray, H., and Pollock, A. B. *Organizational Choice*. London: Tavistock, 1963.

Truzzi, M. (ed.). *Verstehen: Subjective Understanding in the Social Sciences*. Reading, Mass.: Addison-Wesley, 1974.

Vaill, P. B. "The Purposing of High Performing Systems." *Organizational Dynamics*, Autumn 1982, pp. 23–39.

Vaill, P. B. *Managing as a Performing Art: New Ideas for a World of Chaotic Change*. San Francisco: Jossey-Bass, 1989a.

Vaill, P. B. "Seven Process Frontiers for Organization Development." In A. Drexler, W. Sikes, and J. Gant (eds.), *The Emerging Practice of Organization Development*. Alexandria, Va.: NTL Institute, 1989b.

Vaill, P. B. "Executive Development as Spiritual Development." In S. Srivastva, D. L. Cooperrider, and Associates, *Appreciative Management and Leadership: The Power of Positive Thought and Action in Organizations*. San Francisco: Jossey-Bass, 1990.

Vaill, P. B. "Notes on Running an Organization." *Journal of Management Inquiry*, 1992, *1*(2), 130–138.

von Bertalanffy, L. *General Systems Theory: Foundations, Development, Applications*. New York: Braziller, 1969.

Weick, K. E. *The Social Psychology of Organizing*. (2nd ed.) Reading, Mass.: Addison-Wesley, 1979.

Wheatley, M. J. *Leadership and the New Science*. San Francisco: Berrett-Koehler, 1992.

Young, J. Z. *Doubt and Certainty in Science*. New York: Oxford University Press, 1960.

Zaner, R. *The Way of Phenomenology*. New York: Western/Pegasus, 1970.

Zuboff, S. *In the Age of the Smart Machine*. New York: Basic Books, 1988.

Index